CONTEMPORARY
EXHIBIT DESIGN

MARTIN M. PEGLER

VISUAL REFERENCE PUBLICATIONS, INC.—NEW YORK

CBSI

TRADE SHOW—*Internet World, Javitz Center, New York, NY*
DESIGN FIRM—*Exhibitgroup/Giltspur, Chicago, IL*
FABRICATION—*Exhibitgroup/Giltspur, Chicago, IL*
SPACE—*400 sq. ft.*
PHOTOGRAPHY—*Jamie Padgett & Co.*

The 400 sq. ft. display space was dominated by the overhead canopy that reached up and out to bring attention to the software demonstrations that were taking place at ground level. The design of the canopy was actually an abstraction of the client's logo with the red sphere the central focus of the design and there were shiny metal circles radiating out from around the red ball—like orbiting rings around a planet. The three towers that anchored the metal bands supported the client's name and logo and the space appeared to be more spacious due to the towers spreading out overhead. Above eye level messages were delivered on sky blue panels over the metallic table tops. Six demo stations were organized in the minimal space on the aforementioned tabletops.

The warm light colored wood finish which was accented by the metallic trim "echoed CBSI's customer focus" and also "served to demonstrate CBSI's commitment to cutting edge integrated web solutions."

ARTISTIC TILE

CLIENT—*Artistic Tile*

TRADE SHOW—*Architectural Digest Home Design Show,*
   Javitz Center, New York, NY

DESIGNER—*The Displayers, New York, NY*

FABRICATION—*The Displayers, New York, NY*

SPACE—*400 sq. ft.*

PHOTOGRAPHY—*Courtesy of The Displayers*

The challenge for the exhibit designers, The Displayers, was to present 128, 20 in. tile sample boards in a space of 400 sq. ft. and still create a cohesive image for the manufacturer/client. In addition, they had to "make the tile seem light, even weightless, in juxtaposition to the heavy weighted product."

The designers created a double sided hanging system which was not only secure but "sleek and accessible" and the products could be merchandised in numerous ways. The tiles were visible from outside of the exhibit booth. Inside, styled bathroom vignettes were presented along with the "floating" sample tile boards. Seating was also provided for customers in the limited space.

The natural wood framework suggested a friendly, home-style setting and it also complemented the colors and textures of the tiles. MR16 lamps, concealed in the upper framework of the exhibit, highlighted and enhanced the colors of the squares of tiles.

ECAST

CLIENT—*ECAST*

TRADE SHOW—*Amusement & Music Operator Association, Orlando, FL*

DESIGNERS—*Mauk Design, San Francisco, CA*

DESIGN TEAM—*Mitchell Mauk/Laurence Raines*

FABRICATION—*Detail A*

FABRICATION TEAM—*Mark Brown*

SPACE—*400 sq. ft.*

PHOTOGRAPHY—*Laurence Raines*

Ecast invented and sells "internet jukeboxes" to bars and restaurants. Within the 400 sq. ft. allotted, Mauk Design not only had to "explain" the product through actual demonstrations but also make the whole concept a desirable one. "This exhibit needed a design language that could separate and elevate this newcomer from the rest of the established market" and still "maintain a connection with the past."

The silver and gray checkerboard patterned floor became a modern and updated version of the old black and white tiled floors associated with restaurants and bars of decades ago. "Glowing pedestals highlighted the innovative industrial design while the machined aluminum conference room structure pushed towards the future."

The large illuminated cone sat atop the glass enclosed conference room and boldly presented the company's brand name and logo. The conference area had frosted circular graphics on the glass—taken from the product interface—and that provided a sense of privacy. The openings between the panels of glass kept the air circulating.

Through its lighting and the use of innovative form the exhibit made this statement, "We are the future of coin-operated entertainment."

ELITE
GOURMET

CLIENT—*Elkay Manufacturing*

TRADE SHOW—*Kitchen & Bath Industry Show, Orlando, FL*

DESIGNER—*Chicago Exhibit Productions, Bolingbrook, IL*

DESIGN TEAM—*Joe Koziarski*

FABRICATION—*Chicago Exhibit Productions*

LIGHTING—*Tech Lighting*

SPACE—*450 sq. ft.*

PHOTOGRAPHY—*Bruce Wilson Photography*

In a space of 450 sq. ft. the designers, Chicago Exhibit Productions, created two distinct vignettes showing the high end, upscale kitchen components designed by Elkay Manufacturing. The exhibit combined ceramic tile and hardwood flooring along with granite counter tops, wall panels and stainless steel appliances. Sweeping bands of brushed metal carried the brand name above eye level and created pseudo-ceilings for the kitchen settings. In other areas light wood timber was used to form lattice-like "ceilings" over the tile topped counter.

A major challenge for the designers was "to duplicate permanent kitchen constructions in an exhibit that would have to be shipped, installed and dismantled for future use." The design allowed Elkay Manufacturing "to demonstrate to kitchen designers the quality and more importantly—the look—of their new Elite Gourmet line of sinks in actual installations."

DERSE
EXHIBITS

CLIENT—*Derse Exhibits*

TRADE SHOW—*The Exhibitor Show, Las Vegas, NV*

DESIGNER—*Derse Exhibits, Milwaukee, WI*

DESIGN TEAM—*Russ Fowler*

FABRICATION—*Derse Exhibits*

SPACE—*450 sq. ft.*

PHOTOGRAPHY—*Jamie Padgett & Co.*

In an island exhibit area of 18 ft. x 30 ft., Derse Exhibits presented itself at The Exhibitor Show. The focus was to create an environment—rather than an exhibit—which would suggest Derse's "Disney-like creativity" and "NASA-like logistics" to its clients and potential clients. In addition to establishing a physical and visual presence at this show, the exhibit design firm planned to demonstrate three logistic programs and provide space where interested attendees could sit and discuss their problems.

The space was physically defined by two 15 ft. high, dramatically colored, hand painted planes with the Derse brand colors. On the right was the "logistics" area and the "creativity" zone was on the left with the reception counter and information area between. The conference area was situated behind. The exhibit's design also communicated Derse's approach to design and fabrication. 92% of the exhibit was constructed of recyclable materials such as the recycled rubber tiles that were used for the flooring. The walls were aluminum skins on aluminum frames and the conference room was defined by a sheer, mint-tinted fabric. The ceiling canopy was custom modular and also fabricated by Derse.

Computer workstations were placed in the Logistics area while fantasy models, at eye level, were in the Creativity portion of the exhibit along with a portfolio of finished exhibits, a power point presentation of computer renderings on a laptop and "a portfolio of concepts to communicate how our designers think and work."

"Simplicity, immediate impact, and understanding were key to communicating Derse's main objectives—focus on creativity and logistics."

CITICAPITAL

CLIENT—*CitiCapital/CitiGroup*

TRADE SHOW—*Radiological Society of North America, Chicago, IL*

DESIGNER—*MC2, New York, NY*

DESIGN TEAM—*Marissa Kressman*

FABRICATOR—*MC2, New York, NY*

SPACE—*600 sq. ft.*

PHOTOGRAPHER—*Jamie Padgett & Co.*

In an effort to re-brand itself after being acquired by Citigroup, Copelco CitiCapital made its debut with its new look at the RSNA trade show in Chicago. "The goal was to create an image that was distinct and impactful while catering to Citicorp's strict corporate identity lines."

The booth, designed by MC2, covered 600 sq. ft. and made effective use of the CitiGroup's signature colors of blue and white. The colors were enhanced by assorted textural finishes which included brushed aluminum, corrugated plastic and translucent fiberglass. The open circular tower, more than twenty feet off the ground, brought the CitiCapital name and logo into prominence and was easily viewed from anywhere in the hall. At ground level, the circular form was transformed into an on-the-floor-but-apart conference space by means of textured plastic panels.

BBC AMERICA/DISCOVERY COMMUNICATIONS

CLIENT—*BBC America & Discovery Communications, Inc.*

TRADE SHOW—*Western Cable Show, Las Vegas, NV*

DESIGNER—*Exhibitgroup/Giltspur, Seattle, WA*

DESIGN TEAM—*Michael L. Silva*

FABRICATION—*Exhibitgroup/Giltspur, Seattle*

FABRICATION TEAM—*Phil Keane/Tim Jobson/Michael Whitney*

LIGHTING—*Upstaging, Chicago, IL*

SPECIAL PROPS—*Redletter Productions, CA*

SPACE—*600 sq. ft.*

PHOTOGRAPHY—*Jamie Padgett & Co.*

The client's objective which Michael L. Silva and the Exhibitgroup/Giltspur Seattle design team accomplished in the 600 sq. ft. space, was to "capture and portray the BBC brand in three dimensions." The client wanted something that spoke to their image and maintained it through superior craftsmanship and attention to detail.

What made the finished exhibit so unique was the "authenticity of the execution"—with the exception of the photographic cobble-stoned flooring. The fabricators used 8 in. Virginia oak planking for the interior floors and cherry stained birch for the walls. The brick panels were "off-the-shelf," 1/4 in. thick masonite which were enhanced by the artistic application of lighter and darker shades to the brick and the mortar to achieve the desired weathered look. Painted dense cork was used to obtain the asphalt appearance of the "street" and it had a low abrasion factor. One of the especially "fun" features of the design was the use of the rotating silhouette "people" that appeared in one of the upper windows. They were a subtle reference to Benny Hill humor, a man with a cap chasing after a woman in a skirt. The feeling of authenticity combined with the charm and warmth of a British local pub set the scene and the open door invited attendees to enter and enjoy a short stay "abroad."

For a new look and to create a different mood for the same show the following year, this exhibit was repainted a dark blue and was equally effective in accomplishing the client's stated goals.

ECHOPASS

CLIENT—*Echopass, Robert Scorensen*

TRADE SHOW—*Customer Relationship Management (CRM), San Francisco, CA*

DESIGNER—*Steelhead Productions, Poulsbo, WA*

DESIGN TEAM—*Eric Friezen/Ms. Christina, CAD*

FABRICATION—*Steelhead Productions*

FABRICATION TEAM—*John Jorgensen/Scott Vance/Scott Magraw*

LIGHTING DESIGN—*Sean Combs*

AUDIO VISUAL—*McKnight Audio Visual*

SPACE—*600 sq. ft.*

PHOTOGRAPHY—*Jamie Padgett & Co.*

The 600 sq. ft. exhibit designed by Steelhead Productions looked like something out of a space odyssey with steps, arced posts, rings of metal, a glass enclosed capsule and a second story flagship surmounted by a wire framed fabric roof.

To emphasize and dramatically represent Echopass' technology which enables call centers to handle incoming phone inquiries from many services (software and like companies), a live call center was created. Within an elliptical construction of structural grade aluminum and bulletproof lucite panels, four operators took live calls. This was the first time any such tie-in had ever been attempted and actually presented on a trade show floor. The curved flight of open metal stairs lead to the lucite enclosed "neo-modern" conference room atop the call-in center.

The sweeping, curved vertical panels—raised up three steps to a mezzanine level—carried data relevant to the different types of users of Echopass' unique services. A giant cylinder, suspended over the open exhibition area, was illuminated by lighting attached to the aluminum truss circle that surrounded and supported the attention-getting signage.

The colors throughout—white, light blue and black highlighted by metallic accents—were taken from the client's corporate logo which also suggested the bold curves used in the total design.

M C 2

CLIENT—*MC2*

TRADE SHOW—*TS2, McCormick Place, Chicago, IL*

DESIGNER—*MC2, Las Vegas, NV*

DESIGN TEAM—*Jeff Cameron*

FABRICATOR—*MC2, Atlanta, GA*

LIGHTING DESIGN—*Shane Huff, MC2, Atlanta, GA*

AUDIO VISUAL—*Ken Bennett, MC2, Atlanta, GA*

SPACE—*600 sq. ft.*

PHOTOGRAPHY—*Jamie Padgett & Co.*

MC2 was "born" only days before the opening of this TS2 show. MC2 was created when Lincoln Studios and Creative Management Services merged and this show was the new company's debut. The goals for the show were much broader than just simply generating sales leads. "The MC2 brand promise was expressed in our tagline—'the power to shape ideas'"—and Tom Cortese, Senior VP of Marketing said, "Right from the start we wanted prospective clients to view us as a presence marketing solutions provider. We needed our presence at the show to embody the excitement and multidimensional capability we're building into our own brand."

The new MC2 logo appeared everywhere and over and over again to make it at once a recognizable and remembered logo. It appeared in a bold curved expanse of backlit white fabric that rose up to 20 or more feet off the ground and it showed up on TV monitors—at eye level—located around the perimeter of the space. "The design was a lush mixture of texture and tone combining cherry woods, patterned laminates, carpet and slate with powder coated steel and plastic laminates." The plasma monitors were oriented both towards the core of the exhibit and the aisle.

To add an inviting warmth to the environment, translucent materials such as tension fabric and frosted glass were incorporated into the exhibit. The previously mentioned TV monitors were outlined in cherry wood and supported by metallic upright frames that reached up to tie in with the cherry wood "beams" that floated overhead. These beams radiated out from the curved sweep of the tension fabric that was framed in aluminum. Foliage in planters backed up each upright frame to further the gallery ambiance.

A specialized "studio" was included in the total design to demonstrate the company's computer design capabilities and a private conference area was located on the second level with a wood staircase leading up to it.

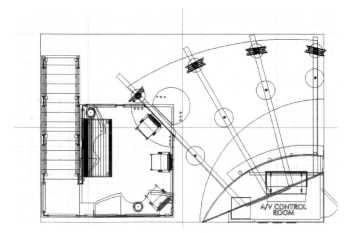

TRANSFORMIT

CLIENT—*Transformit*

SHOW—*GlobalShop 2001, McCormick Place, Chicago, IL*

DESIGNER—*Transformit, NY, Cynthia Thompson*

DESIGN TEAM—*Michael Reidy/Jon Chalfont/Matt Rawdon*

FABRICATION—*Transformit*

FABRICATION TEAM—*Jeff Willis/Ron Remy/Karen
 Eggert/Jonathan Crowe*

LIGHTING—*Michael Reidy/Upstaging*

AUDIO VISUAL—*Tom Faux*

SPACE—*600 sq. ft.*

PHOTOGRAPHY—*Kathy Chapman*

To introduce the new Dreamspinners Collection of free standing fabric walls designed and manufactured by Transformit, the company created their own color-filled environment in a 600 sq. ft. space at the GlobalShop in Chicago. "The enveloping feeling of the structures provided a peaceful retreat from the surrounding chaos of the show of the scale of GlobalShop."

The use of white fabric and the enveloping design "suggested a comprehensive, boutique-like approach" and the uniquely shaped forms and the interlocking nature of the elements with the matching curves' radii enabled these units to be fitted together in a variety of ways. Enriching the all-white construction and the all-white interior furnishings (desk, chairs and floor) were the LED lights and a choreographed sound design which all contributed to the high impact of the display at its location on the show floor. "The exhibit showcased the high

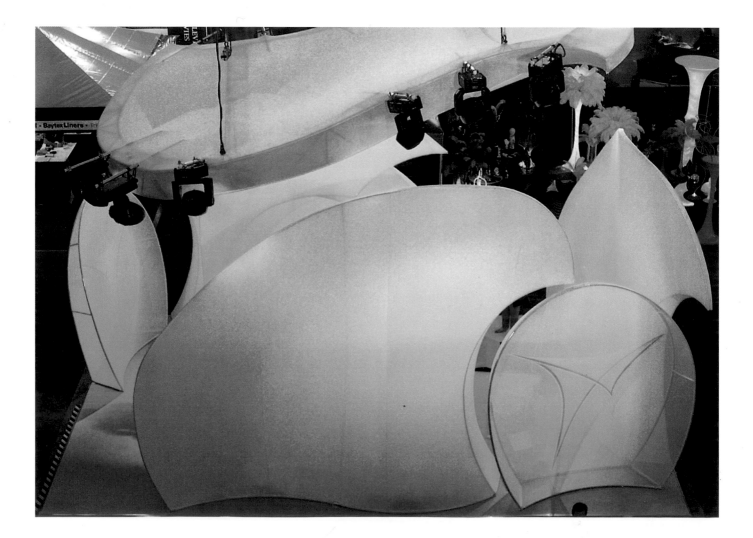

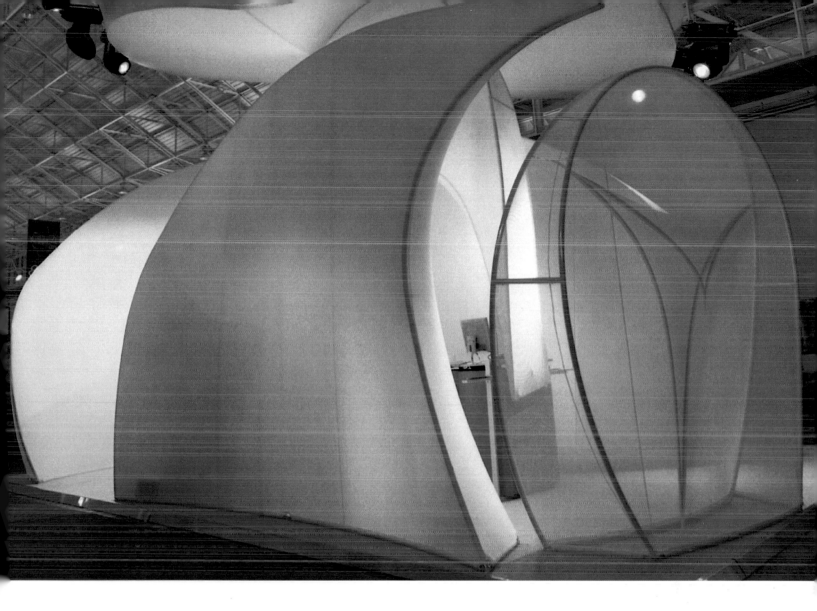

level of craftsmanship and sensitivity to the three dimensional design that Transformit creates."

The booth had defined entrances—for the most part enclosed—with walls blocking the line of sight. "The enclosed design played on the psychology of concealment and the human nature of wanting to see what's inside." The curiosity factor coupled with the defined entrances served as "instant lead qualifiers" and those who "understood" the display, entered. Those who did not—moved on.

The success of the exhibit on a giant floor overflowing with exhibits was proven by its receiving an Award of Merit for Best Booth in Show.

TRANSFORMIT

CLIENT—*Transformit*

TRADE SHOW—*The Special Event, San Diego, CA*

DESIGN—*Transformit, NYC, Cynthia Thompson*

DESIGN TEAM—*Michael Reidy/Jon Chalfont*

FABRICATION—*Transformit, NYC*

FABRICATION TEAM—*Ron Remy/Jeff Willis/Jonathan Crowe/Karen Eggert*

LIGHTING—*Michael Reidy/Upstaging*

AUDIO VISUAL—*Tom Faux*

SPACE—*600 sq. ft.*

PHOTOGRAPHY—*Kathy Chapman*

The entire focus of the 600 sq. ft. space was on the light, movement and sound generated by Transformit's exhibit concept—Blooming Morning Glory—a fabric sculpture that "grows and evolves."

A computer driven, servo-mechanized motor seated in the base of the unit serves to animate the aluminum, tube frame skeletal structure and the Lycra fabric skin. "The sheer size of the moving flower coupled with the imaginative use of a dramatic, theatrical lighting design and soundscape, created considerable positive attention when it was on display." The entire scope of the Blooming Morning Glory project was performed in-house—from the concept and design to the sewing, metal cutting and bending, fabricating the custom connectors, the computerized programming for driving the servo motors which animate the structure, sound design, lighting design and installation.

The "visual excitement" generated by this "multisensory display" attracted many visitors to this booth and made a big scoring point for Transformit as a producer of exciting display elements to integrate into exhibit designs.

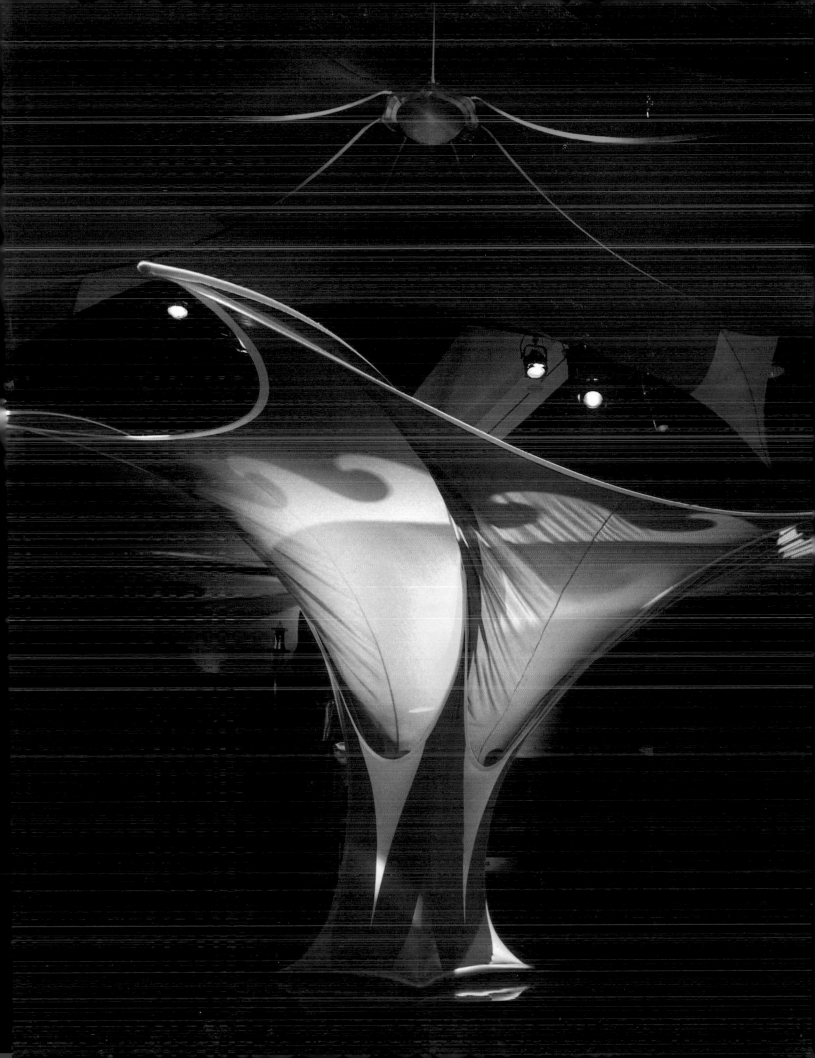

EL PASO GLOBAL NETWORKS

CLIENT—*El Paso Global Networks*

TRADE SHOW—*Internet World, Los Angeles, CA*

DESIGN—*MC2, Atlanta, GA, Tim Rogers*

DESIGN TEAM—*MC2 Atlanta's design team*

FABRICATION—*MC2, Atlanta, GA*

LIGHTING—*MC2/VIP Production*

SPACE—*900 sq. ft.*

PHOTOGRAPHY—*Jamie Padgett & Co.*

To set El Paso Global Networks apart from all the high-tech designs surrounding their 900 sq. ft. space at the Internet World Show, the designers at MC2, Atlanta turned to classic architecture.

The central, focal feature is a circular colonnade with a silk dome atop it. Hanging over the exhibit as "signage" is a giant fabric and wire framed inverted dome that not only carries the brand name but it is alive with changing images and colors. With no actual "products" as such to sell or demonstrations to feature, the designers counted on the architecture, the lights and the video images to introduce and sell the brand name.

Multi-screen presentations told the story and a desk made of truncated Doric columns served as an information center at the open end of the Doric columned colonnade. Simple benches were provided under the animated and activated dome for people who wanted to watch the video presentation. Workstations, similar to the information desks, were set around in the 30 ft. x 30 ft. space and here sales reps met with potential clients. In one corner of the island space a quarter round conference room was located behind a grid wall filled with large panels of lucite. Additional storage space was also situated there.

SOURCEONE
WIRELESS

CLIENT—*Source One Wireless*

TRADE SHOW—*C.E.S., Las Vegas, NV*

DESIGNER—*Derse Exhibits, Milwaukee, WI*

DESIGN TEAM—*Kim Pigeon & Russ Fowler*

FABRICATOR—*Derse Exhibits, Milwaukee, WI.*

SPACE—*900 sq. ft.*

PHOTOGRAPHER—*Show Photography, Courtesy of Derse Exhibits*

The objective in creating this 900 sq. ft. booth for SourceOne Wireless was to aggressively position SourceOne as the provider of the first nationwide calling-party-pays paging service—FOREVERPage. It was also designed to create "high memorability with emphasis on the unique service support."

The design, by Derse Exhibits, is "industry aggressive" in its dynamic use of shapes, materials, lighting and color—even for the C.E.S. show in Las Vegas where it was introduced. The design thrust was to push out to the farthest extremes and still enhance the presentation of the client's lifestyle packaging. Three large seamless 7 ft. x 10 ft. backlit fabric graphics of SourceOne's lifestyle product packaging were used and they promoted the marketing message created by the client's POP design house and their advertising agency. An interactive product show—The Don Philahue Show—attracted substantial audiences to the demonstrations of the FOREVERPager product.

Aluminum frameworks were used within all the structural design shapes thus keeping installation, dismantling and shipping charges at a minimum. The lightweight elements were easily positioned by manual "genie-type" lifts.

MAUI JIM

CLIENT—*Maui Jim*

TRADE SHOW—*Vision Expo, NYC and in Anaheim, CA*

DESIGNER—*Chicago Exhibition Products, Bolingbrook, IL, Joe Koziarski*

FABRICATION—*Chicago Exhibition Productions*

SPECIAL FEATURES—*Polage™ Art by Augustine Wood-Comarow*

SPACE—900 SQ. FT.

PHOTOGRAPHY—*Einzig Photography*

The client, Maui Jim, has been designing, manufacturing and selling high-end fashion sunglasses at moderate prices on the beaches of Maui for over two decades. Now, with 29 styles and patented Polarized Plus® lens technology, the client was set "to spread the spirit of the islands" at trade shows on the mainland. Maui Jim selected Chicago Exhibition Production to design the 900 sq. ft. exhibit space at Vision Expo East, the show that attracts the most prominent retail sunglasses, optical and sport specialty buyers on the East Coast.

The design brought Hawaii to the mainland! The 30 ft. x 30 ft. island was surrounded by floor graphics of a blue ocean and the pale beige carpeting suggested walking on the sand on a beach. Four curved and tapered towers—similar to surfboards—supported the thatch roof which created a tropical cabana atmosphere. Display and workstations were provided and clients could relax and enjoy a cool drink at the juice bar while viewing the effects of the Polarized Plus® technology on the special Polage™ art by Augustine Wood-Comarow. The staff wore Hawaiian shirts custom designed for Maui Jim and music of the Islands filled the "tropical" paradise space.

SAVANE

CLIENT—*Savane International Corp.*
TRADE SHOW—*Magic Show, Las Vegas, NV*
DESIGNER—*Echelon, Arlington Heights, IL*
DESIGN TEAM—*Mark Wagner and design associates*
FABRICATION—*Echelon*
SPACE—*900 sq. ft.*
PHOTOGRAPHY—*Jamie Padgett & Co.*

Throughout, the two level, 900 sq. ft. exhibit designed by Echelon for the Men's fashion company, Savane, exudes a sense of fashion awareness, smart styling and sophistication. Display "windows"—to either side of the gracious opening—suggested an upscale retail store setting and that feeling was carried through inside where the wood floor was used to delineate the separate presentation areas and also lead to the staircase that brought clients to the conference spaces on the upper level.

Natural maple, gun metal laminates and perforated metals were used and they reflected "the image in the brand image." Throughout, black lacquer accents complemented the pale, washed-down birch wood and enhanced the sophisticated, up-end look of the design. Areas of the floor—under the raised conference deck—resembled merchandised bays in a fine men's retail store where the samples were stacked and coordinated much as they would be in any good department or specialty store.

The Savane name and logo was etched into the frosted glass panels that appeared on the sides of the exhibit between the birch wood shadow box windows and the full size display "windows." A giant Savane sign floated over the entrance to the exhibit and it carried through the whitened birch and sharp black color scheme.

IpVERSE

CLIENT—*IpVerse*

TRADE SHOW—*SuperComm 2000, Atlanta, GA*

DESIGN—*Derse Designs, Milwaukee, WI, Jon Horn & staff*

FABRICATION—*Derse Designs*

SPACE—*900 sq. ft.*

PHOTOGRAPHY—*Jamie Padgett & Co.*

The challenge for Derse Design was to create an exhibit to fit the 900 sq. ft. space at SuperComm 2000 which would effectively educate "ISP's on how the SoftSwitch (a software-based switching product) provides an open solution to a wide variety of telecommunications challenges in the new public network." The designers searched for a metaphor around which to design the exhibit that would illustrate the "open architecture" idea with the new public network and IpVerse's SoftSwitch product. The result was an open structure with beams that defined the space. Within the exhibit framework of a custom "whale bone" overhead structure made of 6 in. square tubular aluminum and the tension fabric structures with digital supergraphic branding, the designers placed a live marketing presentation area, demonstration stations, racked equipment as well as a conference area. And yet—throughout the exhibit there was a feeling of "openness and connectivity."

The color scheme of blue and green was carried out. The colors appeared in the blue and sage green carpet inlays, and the sage green and maple laminates used on the signage panels. Cork colored recycled rubber was used as flooring in the raised conferencing area which was semi-obscured by sheer white fabric panels suspended from the angled aluminum ring. Flat plasma monitors also appeared in various parts of the space to add color, excitement and entertainment. The designers succeeded in creating "an exhibit framework whose visual cues subliminally completed the message,"

CRESCENT CARDBOARD

CLIENT—*Crescent Cardboard*

TRADE SHOW—*Art Buyer's Caravan, Javitz Center, New York, NY*

DESIGNER—*Derse Design, Milwaukee, WI*

DESIGN TEAM—*Colm Leon/Ray Gidean of Crescent Cardboard*

FABRICATION—*Derse Design*

SPACE—*1000 sq. ft.*

PHOTOGRAPHY—*Jamie Padgett & Co.*

Crescent is a 100 year old megabrand with high brand recognition and customer loyalty. The firm, producer of cardboards and art mounting supplies, wanted to expand their current brand equity to a position as "a trusted friend" and "a resource to help customers reach their creative goals."

The exhibit designed for them by Derse Design filled the 20 ft. x 50 ft. space in the custom framing/art conservation trade show and it presented the client's products not as color samples on a wall but "as inspirational images in the styles of famous artists of the 20th century and emerging art trends." The open, gallery style environment encouraged interaction based on the "art" and the creative options made possible with Crescent's mat boards and products.

The floor plan of the exhibit separated the ongoing educational seminar area from the selling areas. The open plan and the gallery concept made it easier to cross sell between product lines as well as conclude one interaction while engaging another prospect. The overall design consisted of a series of flowing product galleries with walls finished in two subtle, stucco-like finishes. Unifying the galleries were sweeping headers in copper to "convey a sense of richness consistent with Crescent's reputation for exceptional quality." Adding to the warm, approachable style of the environment was the light colored wood flooring inset into carpeted areas. It also reinforced the gallery atmosphere as did the plants and the excellent, on-target lighting.

B & N

CLIENT—*B&N Industries, Inc.*

TRADE SHOW—*GlobalShop, Chicago, IL*

DESIGN—*B&N Design Staff*

FABRICATION—*Pinnacle Exhibits using B&N's Sorbetti System*

AV DESIGN—*Nakamichi*

SPACE—*1200 sq. ft.*

PHOTOGRAPHY—*Kevin McPhee*

B&N Industries designs and manufactures retail systems that are innovative in structure and aesthetics. For the annual GlobalShop show at McCormick Place in Chicago, the company needed to create a shopper-stopping exhibit for their island space that would not only be dramatic but would also show off their newest retail systems in use.

For the 1200 sq. ft. space the firm's own design team created this bold, clean and color-filled exhibit where most of the construction elements were the company's own systems and products. A giant, 20 ft. high sweeping curve of frosted lucite served as the rear wall of the white floored space and also as the brand signage vehicle that could be seen from almost any vantage point on the busy, noisy floor. The translucent panels were illuminated from within to glow and they also set off all the color Sorbetti fixtures and items that were clustered in groupings around the wall. An aura of light permeated out of the space.

Rather than show off actual merchandise that might detract from the fixtures and forms, the designers used colored glass bottles and beakers and occasional decorative flowers as the "merchandise" with the result that they became part of the smart design of the units and their colors integrated with or complemented the colors of the fixtures. Though other colors were used, the overall impact was the crisp, clean white setting with bright splashes of blue, green and yellow.

"The production process and fresh coloration of the Sorbetti material was a relief from the standard and typical retail fixturing displayed at this show."

IZOD

CLIENT—*Izod Menswear*

TRADE SHOW—*Magic Show, Las Vegas, NV*

DESIGNER—*Echelon, Arlington Heights, IL*

FABRICATION—*Exhibit Partners, Inc.*

SPACE—*1200 sq. ft.*

PHOTOGRAPHY—*Jamie Padgett & Co.*

The noted casualwear manufacturer, Izod, made its stand at the Menswear Magic Show in Las Vegas in this two level exhibit designed by Echelon. The setting was white! In the midst of the color, pizzazz and flashing lights of the Magic Show, this pristine, monochromatic white space loomed not only as clean and contemporary but as "majestic" as well. The white was set off and complemented by the cherry stained wood floor and the steps that lead up to the conferencing space on the mezzanine. Giant supergraphics—backlit and in full color—added sparkle and color highlights to the serene setting and also promoted the products and the "lifestyles" of the targeted market.

The rear wall, at floor level—behind the elliptical shaped information desk and the four columns that supported the portico-like structure—was merchandised to look like an upscale retail men's store. White shelves were stacked with colorful sportswear and they were complemented by the bays with face-out and shoulder-out hung garments. A giant, floor-to-ceiling, glowing graphic really lit up this rear area. The merchandise as well as the exhibit was expertly illuminated by focused canister lighting fixtures and indirect lighting in the retail area.

The under-the-counter lighting on the information desk enhanced the "engraved" Izod logo. The backlit Izod logo also appeared on the two major white walls that created the entrance into the exhibit.

LANDAU & HEYMAN

CLIENT—*Landau & Heyman*

TRADE SHOW—*ICSC 2000, Las Vegas, NV*

DESIGNER—*Tony L Horton Designs, Houston, TX*

DESIGN TEAM—*Tony L. Horton, Principal*
   Gus Hamsho/Krystyna Bojanowski, Architects
   Jerold Thompson/Wayne Keown, Engineers
   Mike Van Pasmel, Graphics Director

FABRICATION—*Tony L Horton Design*

FABRICATION TEAM—*Wayne Keown, VP Production/*
   Don Arient, Prod. Foreman

SPACE—*1200 sq. ft.*

PHOTOGRAPHY—*Aker/Zuonkovic Photographers*

To present the new corporate image of Landau & Heyman at the ICSC show, Tony L Horton Designs created this dignified, rich presence in the 1200 sq. ft. exhibit space. The design was anchored by the 18 ft. tower which featured a pegged, brushed aluminum logo illuminated by concealed neon. This arced pylon could be seen from almost anywhere in the giant hall.

To convey the client's new corporate image, the designers used primarily natural materials and the green "fashion" color to "create a warm yet elegant environment." The arced walls of the curved reception area were finished in a warm white and a soft green accent wall was highlighted by safety glass panels with bleached maple frames "adding to the sophistication of the exhibit." The photographs in the frames showed off the Landau & Heyman properties in a gallery-like manner with each illustration illuminated and outstanding. The same frosty aqua light glow surrounded the top of the receptionist's desk and the cutout letters that stood out from the curved fascia that seemed to swing away from the high tower.

The recessed green painted walls led to the conference areas beyond where clients and representatives could talk in quiet zones.

SILVER
BURDETT
GINN

CLIENT—*Silver Burdett Ginn*

TRADE SHOW—*International Reading Association (IRA),*
New Orleans, LA

DESIGN—*Derse Design, Milwaukee, WI*

DESIGN TEAM—*Jon Horn/Kent Jones*

FABRICATION—*Derse Design*

SPACE—*1200 sq. ft.*

PHOTOGRAPHY—*Courtesy of Derse Design*

Silver Burdett Ginn is a leading publisher of children's textbooks and since they appear at so many different shows a year, they wanted an exhibit that would be flexible and adaptable to a variety of needs and spaces. "The exhibit's modularity would be pushed to the limit to accommodate, often concurrently, 10 ft., 20 ft., 30 ft. and 40 ft. on-lines as well as peninsula booth spaces"

The design, shown here, was used at the IRA show and it filled a 20 ft. x 40 ft. island space plus a 10 ft. x 40 ft. in-line space across the aisle. As designed by Derse Design, the exhibit consisted of three identical 40 ft. in-line exhibits that were configured as a single 20 ft. x 40 ft. with the other 10 ft. x 40 ft. set opposite it. A 17 ft. long by 14 ft. high, double sided sign was located at the center of the booth and it featured logos backlit by high output fluorescent fixtures. Track lighting with multicolored lights set off the "wavy" fabric canopy overhead.

The floor plan contained several freestanding elements including reception counters, two-piece display/storage cabinets, book and activity demonstration carts, and kiosks to display CD Rom programs and videos. To create "learning environments," triangular fabric canopies were supported by pyramid-shaped columns, striped in blue and gray, and the columns had brushed aluminum shelves for product display. The four storage cabinets were 6 ft. long x 4 ft. deep with boldly painted curved fronts and "fun house" doors on the sides. The surface finishes used were a combination of laminates, paints, and bright colored vinyl flooring material. The book carts and kiosks had exposed casters "for additional whimsy and ease of movement."

To connect the two spaces and create the illusion of a single exhibit, Derse created a smaller version of the main overhead sign and this spanned over the aisle. Also unifying the two parts of the exhibit was the overall flooring treatment which combined vinyl material playfully inserted into areas cut out of the carpeting.

PATAGONIA OUTERWEAR

CLIENT—*Eastman Kodak*

TRADE SHOW—*Pavilion, Atlanta Olympicme, Atlanta, GA.*

DESIGN—*Exhibit Group/Giltspur, Rochester, NY*

DESIGN TEAM—*Tim Prinzing, Creative Director*

FABRICATOR—*Exhibit Group/Giltspur, Rochester, NY*

FABRICATION TEAM—*Jim Miller, Operations Manager*

LIGHT & AUDIO DESIGN—*Go Media Productions!!!*

SPECIAL PROPS—*Exhibit Group/Giltspur, Rochester, NY*

SPACE—*20,000 sq. ft.*

PHOTOGRAPHER—*Jamie Padgett*

The objective in creating this 900 sq. ft. booth for SourceOne Wireless was to aggressively position SourceOne as the provider of the first nationwide calling-party-pays paging service—FOREVERPage. It was also designed to create "high memorability with emphasis on the unique service support."

The design, by Derse Exhibits, is "industry aggressive" in its dynamic use of shapes, materials, lighting and color.—even for the C.E.S. show in Las Vegas where it was introduced. The design thrust was to push out to the farthest extremes and still enhance the presentation of the client's lifestyle packaging. Three large seamless 7' x 10' backlit fabric graphics of SourceOne's lifestyle product packaging were used and they promoted the marketing message created by the client's POP design house and their advertising agency. An interactive product show—The Don Philahue Show—attracted substantial audiences to the demonstrations of the FOREVERPager product.

Aluminum frameworks were used within all the structural design shapes thus keeping installation, dismantling and shipping charges at a minimum. The lightweight elements were easily positioned by manual "genie-type" lifts.

VAN HEUSEN

CLIENT—*Van Heusen*

TRADE SHOW—*Magic, Las Vegas, NV*

DESIGN—*Echelon, Arlington Heights, IL*

DESIGN TEAM—*Mike Kelly/Mark Wagner/Jim Kursar*

FABRICATION—*Exhibit Partners, Inc.*

SPACE—*1500 sq. ft.*

PHOTOGRAPHY—*Jamie Padgett & Co.*

"Warm and Woody" describes the Van Heusen 1500 sq. ft. exhibit designed by Echelon for the Magic Menswear show. The designers felt that the success of the design was in the clean and open look—its accessibility.

Considering the action on the floor at the Magic show, this design allowed traffic to flow in from a number of areas and—considering the size of the exhibit—there were numerous areas where interested buyers could sit, look and talk to representatives. On the lower level of the two level construction, a cherry stained central wood aisle led to the rear of the space and to the finely detailed staircases that angled up to the mezzanine where refreshments were served. The staircases, like most of the exhibit, were a clean and contemporary mix of cherry and maple woods accented with stainless steel.

Along the partial walls of the exhibit there were fitted cubicles where the Van Heusen shirts were neatly stacked by color and style for fast and easy presentation. Atop these low, open storage fixtures were angled presentation shelves where examples of the stocked merchandise were displayed at eye level. Set in front of the storage bins and on the patterned pale beige carpet were curved desks with high stools to accommodate the interested attendees. Two standard height desks stood at either side of the staircases and a long work shelf stretched across the rear wall under the giant photomural of the three Van Heusen shirts. Ribbed glass framed in cherry served as dividers and within the frames there were photographs of some of the newest designs. The Van Heusen brand name appeared on a blue field across the front of the raised mezzanine as well as on panels on the front of the exhibit.

TURNBERRY ASSOCIATES

CLIENT—*Turnberry Associates*

TRADE SHOW—*ICSC Show, Las Vegas, NV*

DESIGN—*T L Horton Design, Houston, TX*

DESIGN TEAM—*Tony L. Horton: Principal*

   Krystyna Bojanowski: Architect

   Jerold Thompson & Wayne Keown: Engineers

MIKE VAN PAMEL—*Graphics Director*

FABRICATION—*T L Horton Design*

FABRICATION TEAM—

   Wayne Keown: VP Production

   Alvino Gonzalez & Don Arient: Production Foremen

SPACE—*1500 sq. ft.*

Turnberry Associates' image and its retail portfolio were clearly presented in the 1500 sq. ft. exhibit designed by T L Horton Design. There was a dynamic symmetry in the almost monochromatic design with the bowed receptionist desk centered and the bold, faux marble black and gray tile checkered floor splitting the space into two parts.

Directly behind the receptionist's desk was an opening that was enhanced by the maple wood pilasters on either side and the custom light sconces applied to them. The dark gray wall—in contrast to the warm white walls to either side of the opening—led to the private meeting rooms beyond. Set on one side of the dividing tile aisle on the gray industrial carpeting was a seating cluster of black leather chairs around a maple and glass table. On the other side was a lighter looking table and chairs for chatting and working. The surrounding white walls were accented by the framed, bowed, backlit photos of the Turnberry properties. The overall serene setting was conducive to "serious" business talk.

PACKET VIDEO

CLIENT—*Packet Video*

TRADE SHOW—*CTIA Show, Chicago, IL*

DESIGN—*Exhibitron, National City, CA*

DESIGN TEAM—*Joel Young & Joe Christiana*

FABRICATION—*Exhibitron*

SPACE—*1600 sq. ft.*

PHOTOGRAPHY—*Courtesy of Exhibitron*

Exhibitron designed the exhibit for Packet Video at the CTIA Show and took advantage of the 1600 sq. ft. space to spread out—open up—and really allowed interested attendees to enter and move freely about and discover what Packet Video was all about.

A sweeping, all-enveloping wire frame and fabric covered swirl was emblazoned over and over again with the client's name, and it served to contain and also crown the exhibit space. The uppermost ring could be seen from a distance. To create "a subtle contemporary look and feel," deep brown wood, accented with black and stainless steel, was used for the various demonstration stations. Curved partial walls of black laminate served as private meeting areas on the open floor. A special "theater" which could seat 15, was set aside behind a wall of wood gridded in metal. Live demonstrations that drew numerous visitors were performed here. The overall effect was "inviting."

ONSTAR
BATMAN CAVE

CLIENT—*OnStar*

TRADE SHOW—*Texas State Fair*

DESIGN & FABRICATION—*The George P. Johnson Co., Auburn Hills, MI*

DESIGN TEAM—*Norm Liljegren & Valentino Fischione*

SPACE—*1500 sq. ft.*

PHOTOGRAPHY—*Jeff Granbery*

The objective for the George P. Johnson Co. of Auburn Hills, MI was to meld into a single "memorable and compelling" unit exhibit architecture/design, special effects and interactive communication that would attract and excite the visitors to this 1500 sq.ft. exhibit space at the Texas State Fair. "The use of interactive video Batman/OnStar games located on the kiosks, plasma screen monitors showing OnStar commercials and computer controlled gobo projectors that sweep the space and focus the OnStar or Batman logos at predetermined locations including an overhead projection membrane, aided in the technological innovation of this exhibit."

The designers created the bizarre, fantasy-like setting of Gotham City in a blend of "future and boilerplate

technology." A fog machine, concealed in the molded fiberglass cave backwall of the exhibit, spread a blanket of mysterious mist over the attention-getting Batmobile platform—"creating a sense of drama and intrigue." The "urban" feeling was enhanced by the concrete texture and metal grating accented with nuts, bolts and rivets while the faux artwork of scenic artists replicated rusty and weathered metal. "Concrete" pylons over 17 ft. tall, were used to break up the amorphous rock and stalagmite formations of the "cave" and the verticals carried the plasma

monitors and the speakers for the sound system. These strong, vertical elements were decorated with illuminated OnStar and Batman logos. Other elements introduced in recreating the decaying Gotham City infrastructure included a rusty water main pipe with shut-off valve and a decrepit steel ladder bolted on to one of the pylons.

Additional interest was created with an illuminated showcase for Batman movie memorabilia including a mannequin in the actual Batman outfit. At the information desk there were brochures available as well as any needed information.

BADSF

CLIENT—*Bay Area Display, San Francisco, San Francisco, CA*

TRADE SHOW—*GlobalShop 2001, McCormick Place, Chicago, IL*

DESIGN—*BADSF*

DESIGN TEAM—*Jacques Casamajor & Elizabeth Baena*

FABRICATION—*BADSF, George Ramirez*

SPACE—*1600 sq. ft.*

PHOTOGRAPHY—*Courtesy of BADSF*

Bay Area Display San Francisco has been a leading designer/manufacturer of fixtures, mannequin alternatives and decoratives for the retail industry for over 50 years. Each year, at GlobalShop, BADSF makes a strong presence with its unique and always different exhibit and the presentation of the new designs.

For GlobalShop 2001, Ron Rodriguez, CEO and President of BADSF, wanted something totally different and something that would "have a positive effect on the environment." The final concept was to design an exhibit that would be "totally recyclable and reusable, using common, inexpensive materials in a unique way." Designers Jacques Casamajor and Elizabeth Baena came up with a clean constructivist design involving a closed

booth with 10 ft. and 20 ft. high walls, wide openings, randomly placed windows accented with color for prominence, and an expansive interior space "recalling a walled-in courtyard."

The designers, after much research, decided on using corrugated cardboard treated with a nontoxic flame retardant for the "skin" over a steel framework. Durable, reusable roll linoleum covered the floor, and the doorways and windows were edged in red. Packaging tape was used to seal the seams so that the finished exhibit looked somewhat like a giant shipping carton. "The extensive use of cardboard with its warm color and surface texture created a soothing environment" and the natural, raw finish "played on the perceptions of value" putting the focus on the product

presentation rather than the exhibit. In a way, the over-scaled "carton" also suggested that BADSF designs, makes and ships display products.

BADSF teamed up with Chicago's Resource Center and after the show the modular cardboard panels were removed and shipped to the Resource Center which has a comprehensive recycling and reuse program. The panels were made available to local schools and artists to create new art projects. Thus, the material reuse solution that Ron Rodriguez sought, was found. The exhibit's originality and effective design was acknowledged with a Best in Show exhibit award.

WORLD WIDE PACKETS

CLIENT—*World Wide Packets*

TRADE SHOW—*Comdex 2000, Las Vegas, NV*

DESIGN—*Exhibitgroup/Giltspur, Southwest*

DESIGN TEAM—*Philip Lawson/Sarah Randall/Doug Wenzel*

FABRICATION—*Exhibitgroup/Giltspur, Southwest*

FABRICATION TEAM—*Larry Shoop/Jerry Meeks/Rich Anselmo*

SPACE—*1600 sq. ft.*

PHOTOGRAPHY—*Jamie Padgett & Co.*

A series of cylinders, tubes and circular forms set the look for the World Wide Packets exhibit designed by Exhibitgroup/Giltspur's Southwest division. The 1600 sq. ft. exhibit was introduced at Comdex 2000 and within its circles and cylinders were contained conference space, quiet zones, food service and special exhibits. Since this was a very new company, the "space age" design executed in cool blue, sharp yellow and white made a strong impact on the show floor.

The main, massive two story high cylinder, with a superstructure of signage and branding above it, was covered with words and graphic messages. Riding around the circumference on a bright yellow track was a miniature train—also yellow—that tied-in with the client's involvement with trains. Work stations became satellites

of the main structure as did a private conference room behind fabric mesh panels.

Shooting out of and off the focal central structure were giant plastic tubes girded with metal rings—like heroic scaled pneumatic tubes. In addition, tinker-toy-like extensions from the cylinder, with holes evenly spaced, carried aluminum pipes that extended over the

screened-in, semicircular conference area. Video monitors and plasma screens were integrated into the various work stations to involve and entertain the interested attendees.

Throughout, the silvery metallic accents and elements and the subtle gray areas further enhanced the blue, yellow and white colors of World Wide Packets' signage/logo.

JOHNSTON
& MURPHY

CLIENT—*Johnston & Murphy Footwear*

TRADE SHOW—*World Shoe Association, Las Vegas, NV*

DESIGNER—*Echelon, Arlington Heights, IL*

DESIGN TEAM—*Mark Wagner*

FABRICATOR—*Exhibit Partners, Inc.*

SPACE—*2000 sq. ft.*

PHOTOGRAPHER—*Jamie Padgett & Co.*

The handsome 2000 sq. ft. exhibit space designed for Johnston & Murphy by Echelon was an instant image maker. What the exhibit designers hoped to accomplish and succeeded at was to render the look and quality of the client's brand image as expressed in their new flagship store on Madison Ave. in New York City. As in that store, the grand staircase plays an important part in creating the upscale, sophisticated yet masculine environment for Johnston & Murphy's shoes and accessories. "The success of the design can be attributed to the fact that it identified with and furthered the aesthetic of the client's branding."

The exhibit provided both private presentation areas or conference spaces with the wide, open spaciousness of the ground level viewing. A small "shop-within-the-shop" enhanced the feeling of being inside the actual flagship store. In many ways the space was "majestic" but still "warm, welcoming and inviting" thanks to the extensive use of maple wood, maple veneer, maple moldings, fluted glass and the wrought iron railing. Another key element to the overall effectiveness of the design was the appropriate lighting on the product as well as the ambient lighting that suggested an in-store shopping experience in the midst of a trade show surrounding.

ROADRANGER

CLIENT—*Eaton/Dana Corp., a joint venture*

TRADE SHOW—*Mid Atlantic Trucking Show, Louisville, KY*

DESIGN—*Derse Exhibits, Milwaukee, WI*

DESIGN TEAM—*Jon Horne/John Melse*

FABRICATION—*Derse Exhibits*

SPACE—*2000 sq. ft.*

PHOTOGRAPHY—*Jamie Padgett & Co.*

The "Roadranger," which represented the new brand created by the marketing merger between Eaton and Dana Corp., was introduced in an exhibit designed by Derse Exhibits and presented in a 40 ft. x 50 ft. space at the Mid Atlantic Trucking Show. Strong, flying fabric and aerodynamic shapes appeared overhead to bring attention to the brand name. The largest one brought special attention to "The Drivetrain"—the exhibit's flagship display which combined all of the Eaton and Dana products and was thus the heart of "Roadranger." Appearing over the actual drivetrain, on a 40 in. plasmavision screen, was a fast-paced TV spot that looped periodically.

To show how Roadranger supported the hardware with the less tangible efforts of their superior service and engineering, six graphic marketing messages or "value drivers" were visible at eye-level on a second tier. "They created a directional rhythm that moved the attendees through the space." The supergraphics were digitally imprinted on fabric skins that fit over lightweight frames. Fabric canopies and low voltage lighting overhead "created mini-environments that helped to focus individual attention." In addition, product and service logos were projected onto the floor and all about the space while the centrally located dual function website and general infor-

mation interactive station also provided a contemporary, high tech image.

Without distracting from the Roadranger message, the client also wanted to introduce "The Lightening Transmission." This was introduced in "the second hottest corner of the space and injected some product display steroids." Looped PVD showings of the on-the edge new Lightening campaign video were played on three plasmavision screens around the base of the display.

"Don't touch the rail—You might get shocked"— helped draw attendees closer to the screens.

Using lightweight materials such as tension fabric, graphics and aluminum skeletal interiors with translucent fiberglass skins, the designers were able to produce an exhibit half the weight of its predecessor and also brought down all logistic costs. "At the same time, the experience one feels in this environment truly creates a paradigm-shift for this market."

BROADMAN & HOLMAN

CLIENT—*Broadman & Holman Publishing*

TRADE SHOW—*Christian Booksellers Association, Dallas, TX*

DESIGN—*Derse Exhibits, Milwaukee, WI, Jon Horn*

FABRICATION—*Derse Exhibits, C. Chris Smith*

SPACE—*2400 sq. ft.*

PHOTOGRAPHY—*Courtesy of Derse Exhibits*

For over a century Broadman & Holman have been well known and highly respected publishers of quality Bibles and related Christian books, products and services. With a desire to move into new market areas and the need to appear at more shows and often in different size spaces, they approached Derse Exhibits to create a new, modular exhibit which could adapt from 10 ft. x 10 ft. in-line spaces to 60 ft. x 60 ft. islands.

The first impression the show attendee got was of two 26 ft. tall "halo" canopy topped towers illuminated from within by hi-output lighting. They not only supported the corporate identity in cool blue but also had a deco-styled window elements. These "beacons" also functioned, at their bases, as a storage closet on one side and a conference area that could accommodate six on the other side.

A raised platform in the center of the exhibit served to define the reception and conferencing environments. Internally-lit product showcases were recessed into the maple floors—near the aisles—to act as "audience grabbers." Towering bookcover supergraphics—7 ft. wide x 16 ft. tall—were dye-sublimation prints on spandex fabric that was stretched over aluminum frames and these winged panels were illuminated from below by hi-output fixtures recessed in the raised platform.

By using "pivoting leg kiosks," more product was on display than had been previously possible with the usual gondola-style bookshelves. The custom designed "dashed-slot" panels turned on their central leg thus providing the optimum viewing angle from the aisle. They also had featured product end caps with curved face Duratrans. Products were highlighted by track lighting on the curved overhead beam.

The space, as set up in this 2400 sq. ft. space allowed for ten semiprivate selling environments and two additional 10 ft. x 10 ft. feature product areas which, in this configuration, linked the in-lines with the main island area. The selling alcoves provided the sales staff with product, storage, audiovisual demonstrations and lap top computers for order writing, and an under counter printer output. Hi-output fixtures on the tops of the cabinets provided the light that bounced off the overhead canopy wings. In addition to making this a successful showing for the client, the exhibit also won a Best in Show award for its category.

TRW

CLIENT—*TRW*

TRADE SHOW—*SAE Congress, Detroit, MI*

DESIGN—*Exhibitgroup/Giltspur, Pittsburgh, Steve Snow*

DESIGN TEAM—*Michael Berrey/Jihn Henken*

FABRICATION—*Exhibitgroup/Giltspur, Pittsburgh*

AUDIO VISUALS—*City Animation, Detroit, MI*

SPACE—*2400 sq. ft.*

PHOTOGRAPHY—*Jamie Padgett & Co.*

TRW's 2400 sq. ft. exhibit at the SAE Congress made an impactful statement on the show floor. Designed by Michael Berrey and the Exhibitgroup/Giltspur's Pittsburgh division, the sharp, almost monochromatic red color with brushed metal accents underscored the "leading edge architecture" of the bi-level structure which contained conference areas, food service and assorted special exhibits.

A bold sweep of red set off the main structure and up front, off the aisle, there was the information desk made of brushed metal and the TRW logo was prominently displayed. The desk was backed up by as giant plasmavision screen which added action and entertainment as well as product display for those who waited to be served. Partially hidden, but still visible, was the staircase that led to the upper level where a series of semiprivate conferencing setups were located. Semi-translucent fabrics, stretched on metal frames, served as dividers between the spaces as well as "walls" along the outer perimeter that toned down the distracting sounds, sights and lights from the show floor.

The lower level exhibit areas contained museum-type demonstration areas featuring the company's steering, braking and airbag systems as well as live demonstrations that attracted audiences and soon involved them in the assorted clearly-identified displays. The openness of the plan was conducive to attendees entering from many directions and having the freedom to move about as they pleased.

TEVETEN

CLIENT—*Solvay Pharmaceuticals*

TRADE SHOW—*American Heart Association, Atlanta, GA*

DESIGN—*Exhibitgroup Giltspur, Atlanta, GA*

DESIGN TEAM—*Mark Burns/Bill Hodgson
  Scott Tniews/Tim Kelley*

FABRICATION—*Exhibitgroup/Giltspur, Atlanta*

LIGHTING—*Intelecon*

AUDIO-VISUALS—*Vantage Point Imaging & Intelecon*

SPACE—*2500 sq. ft.*

PHOTOGRAPHY—*Jamie Padgett & Co.*

The exhibit created for Solvay Pharmaceuticals to introduce their new product—Teveten—at the American Heart Association show in Atlanta also had to reinforce Solvay's corporate identity. As designed by the Atlanta division of Exhibitgroup/Giltspur, the 2500 sq. ft. exhibit established immediate recognition at the entrance to the space by flashing a series of the client's familiar identity images (semi-abstract, modern paintings of heart-shaped faces) on suspended flat screen monitors.

Visitors were then directed through a "vascular" tunnel which featured a beating heart. The "tunnel" was created of tension fabric pulled taut over the white metal pipe formed semi-round arches. The floor, here, was covered in an earthy orange vinyl material. Touch screens within the tunnel provided educational material on the benefits of the drug. Rising like a wave up from the tunnel is a white fabric covered framework canopy that received colored light images and also carried the Teveten name in blue letters high above the exhibit floor.

Interested persons could then withdraw to "living room-like" conference areas in the central part of the exhibit where soft black leather chairs with corner tables were grouped on the light colored wood floor. Adding to the overall relaxed and inviting ambiance of the exhibit was the "calming" music, the soft background sounds and the soft lighting directed towards the center of the almost circular exhibit. The artist who created the original artwork that appeared on the company's brochure was in attendance to sign posters for the attendees. "The exhibit was designed to make the doctors feel comfortable both in entering to learn more about the drug through education and then in prescribing the drug Teveten."

ALU

CLIENT—*ALU*

SHOW—*GlobalShop 1999, Chicago, IL*

DESIGN—*ALU, New York*

DESIGN TEAM—*Erwin Winkler/Massimo Bianchi/*
   Tom Usinowicz

FABRICATION—*ALU*

AUDIO VISUAL—*Bose*

SPACE—*3000 sq. ft.*

PHOTOGRAPHY—*Massimo Bianchi*

The color orange—strong and unabashed—distinguished the ALU booth at the GlobalShop Show in the vast McCormick Place in Chicago. Orange and white—white and orange; it was the dramatic use of the high visibility color and the beakers and laboratory flasks filled with orange liquid showed off ALU's newest structural/display/fixture systems at a show filled with awe inspiring new revelations.

Erwin Winkler, president of ALU, decided "to show our systems in a distinctly architectural environment. ALU's designs meld seamlessly with pre-built environments." The exhibit, designed by ALU's designers, consisted of two huge orange colored curved walls that extended in excess of 20 ft. and they were surrounded by square white pylons—8 ft. tall—with illuminated shadow boxes set in them. The entrance to the semi-enclosed exhibit was between these displays. The 12 ft. orange panels set to either side of the entry carried TV monitors that relayed images of the company's products.

The exterior of the exhibit was divided into display vignettes in which ALU's assorted fixture systems were shown in various configurations and the laboratory equipment served as the product display. The strong "spiritually inspired minimalistic" architectural feeling of the exhibit contrasted with but also enhanced the lightness and airy feeling of the assorted aluminum products and systems.

SYMA

CLIENT—*Syma Systems, AG*

TRADE SHOW—*EuroShop '99, Dusseldorf, Germany*

DESIGN—*Syma Expo*

FABRICATION—*Syma Systems, AG, Switzerland*

SPACE—*3000 sq. ft.*

PHOTOGRAPHY—*Ivan Eberle*

The superspectacular space fantasy that filled the 280 sq. meters (3000 sq. ft.) exhibit space at the EuroShop '99 in Dusseldorf was all Syma. Syma Systems AG of Switzerland has for many years been one of the leading designers/manufacturers of structural and fixture/fitting systems. For the tri-annual trade show which brings attendees with interests in store design, fixturing and display from all over the world, the company designed this several story high creation.

All silvery, metallic and glowing with light was this high-tech design constructed with Syma systems. The unique shapes and forms that were evolved for the graceful, soaring elliptical fins that anchored three corners of the island space as well as the main structure filled with curves, arcs and angles, were all a tribute to the many possible uses of the product. The construction details were "explained" in the pylons where viewers could study, up close, how the company's component elements went together. A huge superstructure of aluminum pipes connected the three pylons to the main structure—overhead—to delineate the actual space of the exhibit.

Within the main construction there were conference areas, food service and additional quiet zones for major meetings. There were space oriented desks and stools that seemed more in tune with futuristic images of things to come. Out on the floor there were many smaller constructions showing the various systems in use as fixtures, as display modules, as platforms and screens. Lighting from hi output lamps flooded the space while the building itself was equipped with ceiling spots and track lighting.

JOHN PAUL MITCHELL

CLIENT—*John Paul Mitchell Systems*

TRADE SHOW—*Midwest Beauty Show, Rosemont, IL*

DESIGNER—*Displayworks, Irvine, CA*

DESIGN TEAM—*Ray Kunar/Jennifer Campbell/Don
  Hones/Randy Burk*

FABRICATION—*Displayworks*

SPACE—*3500 sq. ft.*

PHOTOGRAPHY—*Jamie Padgett & Co.*

Displayworks designed the new 3500 sq. ft. exhibit for John Paul Mitchell Systems to use at the Midwest Beauty Show. The exhibit combined a retail sales area with an image building presentation of the John Paul Mitchell beauty products. A 16 ft. x 16 ft. elliptical tower loomed up over the space to proclaim the location of the John Paul Mitchell exhibit while also serving to unify the various elements of the exhibit that seemed to radiate out from it. Using a black and white color scheme, the oversized photo blowups added interest and color to the space as did the always "on" TV monitors which were located throughout the space. Products were on display on glass shelves and in large "floating" plexiglass spheres where new products were introduced and featured. A series of metal framed, self-standing units were designed that combined the curved brushed metal supports with the rich,

deep mahogany wood bases. The back wall starred a giant photo enlargement of the John Paul Mitchell ads and the outriggers, on top, supported a framework that carried the brand name. At either end of each unit—up front—stood a trio of the previously mentioned spheres with the featured products. In some cases a white laminate and metal trimmed counter was set in front, on the aisle, and more products were shown on the table top.

A main feature of the exhibit was a 16 ft. diameter stage where live demonstrations were presented at specified intervals. When not in use, an illuminated tube dropped down over the stage.

SGI

CLIENT—*Silicon Graphics, Inc.*

TRADE SHOW—*Siggraph '99, Los Angeles, CA*

DESIGNER—*Landor Associates, San Francisco, CA*

DESIGN TEAM—*Scott Drummond/Jean Loo/
John Trotter/Ivan Thelin*

FABRICATION—*Displayworks*

SPACE—*3600 sq. ft.*

PHOTOGRAPHY—*Jeff Johnson & Eric Harvey of
Landor Associates*

"White is an important element in the new SGI identity system, and one of our greatest challenges was to uphold the spirit of the visual identity while developing a three dimensional solution appropriate for trade show venues." With that in focus, Landor Associates designed this prize winning exhibit for Silicon Graphics, Inc. which appeared at the Siggraph '99 Show.

Since another challenge was to design exhibit modulars that could accommodate multiple products and demon-

stration needs, the designers created a series of units which would allow for expansion or contraction depending upon the trade show floor space. These modules could fit spaces from 20 ft. x 20 ft. up to 60 ft. x 60 ft.—as shown here. There was an illuminated 24 ft. tower that acted as the booth marker and the individual demonstration pods that allowed buyers to experience hands-on interaction with the various SGI systems. The final element was a circular station area that accommodated large groups for purposes of live demonstrations.

It was the new "friendlier, rounder typeface" of SGI's new logo that "set the tone for the exhibit design language." The designers created the minimalist style exhibit to serve as a "blank palette"; the color palette furthered the identity system—emphasizing the white—and color accents appeared in the graphic panels and identity elements that comple-

mented the products on display. The neutral background also accentuated SGI's sculptural monitors and hard drives.

Instead of a specific traffic pattern, attendees were allowed to wander. "We didn't have a linear path; we wanted the floor plan to be free-flowing so attendees could go from space to space." The demonstration stations and graphics served as "visual markers." Some graphic panels were purple, blue and green—to coordinate with the demo areas. They created a "field of color and a visual sightline." By designing curves into the demo stations, it enabled them to be linked together back to back or side by side. "The demo stations create a feel of texture in the exhibit."

"The exhibit is fresh, colorful and dramatic—yet functional enough to work in a trade show setting." The judges agreed and awarded the exhibit the gold award in the island category at that show.

LUCENT TECHNOLOGY

CLIENT—*Lucent Technology*

TRADE SHOW—*Comnet, Washington Convention Center, VA*

DESIGNER—*Exhibitgroup/Giltspur, NY*

DESIGN TEAM—*Mihri Kim—lead designer*

   Kelly Schenker & Dawn Cornell: Graphic Design

   Fabrication: Exhibitgroup/Giltspur, NY

   Fabrication Team: Betsy Ruster/Karen Murray/Russell

     Winters/Gene Tunney/Steve Cashour/Lee Haase

LIGHTING—*Intelecon*

SPACE—*3600 sq. ft.*

PHOTOGRAPHY—*Jamie Padgett & Co.*

Instead of their "traditional" look, Lucent Technology approached the New York division of Exhibitgroup/Giltspur and requested an exhibit that would be "unique, practical, eye-catching-and modular" in design. Also, the design would have to transmit the marketing message that Lucent is a worldwide leader in telecommunications. The 3600 sq. ft. booth appeared at the Comnet Show and the concept, by Mihri Kim, consisted of " basic geometry." It all started with a simple graphic composition of a triangle and a circle which was used both in plan and elevation and the "simple but unique" look was transferred into the layout of the booth. The circle was used to recall the Lucent logo while the wedges and triangles represented Lucent's cutting edge technology.

Since there were several product stations set up in the exhibit area, and the repetition of the shapes of the stations established a look, the design of the product station was critical for the design. The designer came up with "a simple shape that followed the function." "It followed the same wedgy forms of the walls and ceiling and created a rhythm that unified the exhibit." A computer and graphic message in each station successfully blended and created a unique marketing device to promote the Lucent product.

Most of the exhibit was done in off-white—Lucent's color. Lighting added the color and the excitement and also helped to delineate the various stations. The focal point of the booth's layout was the infrastructure wall which had a very strong graphic appeal. Since the exhibit would be used again—possibly in different size spaces—the modularity of the design made it possible to rearrange and reposition the elements into configurations that would work in the selected spaces and still keep the same visual impact; "a new, innovative, sharp image of the leader in the telecommunications industry."

NOKIA ICEBERG

CLIENT—*Nokia*

TRADE SHOW—*PSC, Dallas, TX*

DESIGNER—*Exhibitgroup/Giltspur*

DESIGN TEAM—*David Liau/Steven Levesque/Chris Walters*

FABRICATION—*Exhibitgroup/Giltspur and DDS*

LIGHTING—*Brian O'Connor*

SPACE—*4200 sq. ft.*

PHOTOGRAPHY—*Jamie Padgett & Co.*

Nokia, a Finnish company, selected Exhibitgroup/ Giltspur to create the 4200 sq. ft. exhibit that appeared at the PSC Show in Dallas. What helped finally impress the buyers that Nokia was Finnish and not Japanese, as previously perceived, were the fabulous 20 ft. high icebergs that dominated the space and made the total display so unusual.

DDS, a division of Exhibitgroup/Giltspur of Dallas, created these giant icebergs carved by hand from foam and then "skinned" with a resilient rubber coating. Bathed in chilling blue light, the icebergs took on an even icier glow and the first pair carried the Nokia signage up front. Other icebergs were used further into the exhibit space and they were contrasted with the framed stretched

fabric elements that reinforced the brand name while leading buyers into the warmer, friendlier and more inviting "lodge-like" interior where they could see and actually try the company's phones.

Scandinavian styled fixtures and cases of light natural woods showcased the Nokia products while "surfboard-like" wooden demo stations featured some of the newer designs on lucite shelves. Built-in spots highlighted them and invited the visitors to pick one up and try it.

Computers were lined up on a wood shelf and they were available to shoppers interested in getting more information. The Nokia blue information cards were "embedded" in the "snowbanks" that pushed in below the shelf. Panels of stretched translucent fabric served as subtle dividers that also created a traffic pattern through the inner exhibit area which also included conferencing areas and quiet zones.

AGERE

CLIENT—*Agere Systems*

TRADE SHOW—*Optical Fiber Conference, Anaheim, CA*

DESIGNER—*MC2, Las Vegas, NV, Todd Sussman*

FABRICATION—*MC2, Las Vegas & Chestnut Ridge*

LIGHTING—*Gerry Azoulay at MC2 & David Rees, JCR Production Service*

AUDIO VISUAL—*Gerry Azoulay*

SPACE—*4500 sq. ft.*

PHOTOGRAPHY—*Jamie Padgett & Co.*

Since Agere is a spin-off of Lucent Technologies and it was making its debut at the Optical Fiber Conference in Anaheim, it was important that the exhibit "quickly build brand identity and establish the reputation of an industry leader." To make that impact, the company took 4500 sq. ft. at the show and commissioned MC2 of Las Vegas to create a design that would sell the name, the product and also educate the buying public.

The sophistication of the Agere products was immediately established by the subtle and smart color palette of black, purple, and gray and the use of soft curves and translucent canopies. The circle motif that appears in the "g" in the Angere logo inspired the repeated and very

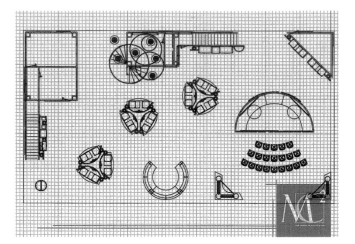

effective use of the circle throughout the design. Circles appeared like floating bubbles on the black outer facade of the exhibit and they were filled with full color illustrations of Agere products. Inside the exhibit the circle motif was repeated in the circular and semicircular booths and the demo stations set out on the gray carpet which was accented with giant purple dot inlays.

A semicircular element, over 20 ft. high and quite wide, served as the background for the stage where live demonstrations were presented. Several dozen viewers could be accommodated comfortably while many more could find standing room and watch. The designers used "Synergy"—a rental system they developed and fabricated to furnish the space.

CENTURY SPORTING GOODS

CLIENT—*Century Sporting Goods*

TRADE SHOW—*The Super Show, Las Vegas, NV*

DESIGNER—*MC2, Atlanta, Brian Baker, designer*

FABRICATION—*MC2, Atlanta*

LIGHTING—*Shane Huff of MC2*

SPACE—*4800 sq.ft.*

PHOTOGRAPHY -*Jamie Padgett & Co.*

"We look at the Super Show as the opportunity to create a temporary showroom that will be visited by all of our clients. With so many products, some of which are large and difficult to transport, this is our only opportunity to show our sporting goods retailer clients the entire breadth of our line," said Cary Williford, VP of Sales and Marketing for Century Sporting Goods. The firm has been in existence for over a quarter of a century and this show provided them with the capability and the audience to present their new, sleeker corporate ID in a contemporary and sophisticated setting.

MC2's Atlanta division fashioned the 4800 sq. ft. exhibit like a high-end sporting goods department store with each zone or area focusing on a different aspect of Century Sporting Goods' product line. The focal point of the exhibit was a 15 ft. high purple wall that serpentined diagonally through the space. The color purple appears on the company's newer marketing materials and it "added a passionate and sexy character to the environment." "We wanted more drama," said Brian Baker, MC2's designer, "and purple gave us that quality while adding warmth and closeness appropriate to a home product." Applied to this snaking wall was a 6 ft. high

company logo and the wall also separated the exhibit into individual areas while creating a traffic pattern that led attendees through the exhibit.

To accentuate the specific product areas, 15 ft. high by 4 ft. wide purple duotone photographs were incorporated into the design as "signage." Grid wall and other retail merchandising systems were used to create the "retail setting" for the product displays thus showing retailers how these products could be presented in their own stores.

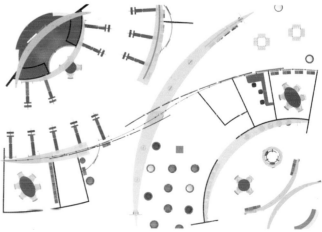

A small stage was located at the corner of the exhibit area which faced the traffic aisle and thus received the highest foot traffic. New products were demonstrated here at ten minute intervals and a live, closed circuit feed was run from the stage to plasma screens strategically placed elsewhere in the exhibit so that buyers anyplace in the exhibit environs could see what was going on. Said Cary Williford of Century Sporting Goods, "The exhibit layout worked in leading our customers through the various product areas and they took the time to see everything we've got."

CRAVE ENTERTAINMENT

CLIENT—*Crave Entertainment/SVG*

TRADE SHOW—*E3, 2000, Las Vegas, NV*

DESIGNER—*Derse Exhibits, Milwaukee, WI*

FABRICATION—*Derse Exhibits*

SPACE—*5000 sq. ft.*

PHOTOGRAPHY—*Courtesy of Derse Exhibits*

E3 is a super special, super spectacular trade show where ENTERTAINMENT in all its many aspects is the central focus. Crave Entertainment, as the name suggests, designs and manufactures video games for the Entertainment industry and SVG is a video game distributor.

For the 2000 show in Las Vegas, Crave commissioned Derse Exhibits to design an exhibit that would fit into the 5000 sq. ft. space and which would give both companies their own individual presence while also introducing the new games. The exhibit had to also have entertainment/demo stations that could be adapted to other spaces—such as stores in malls. All of this had to happen in a fun and amus-

ing environment that would attract people and specifically relate to Crave's and SVG's games.

Two entrances were created for the exhibit with different graphic identities. A second deck was added to accommodate special themed areas as well as a casual selling area. Walkways between the decks gave visitors an "overview" of the entire exhibit layout. To add excitement and generate a theatrical quality for the experience, special lighting effects were introduced and gobos, synchronized with video and sound, provided addition pizzazz. To promote the new game titles of each company and also to underscore the presence of these "players," large digital graphics appeared throughout along with figures and 3-D game parts that extended out from the walls.

Game pods were designed by Derse that could contain three game stations and these pods could later be used, free standing, in malls and game arcades. Each pod also included literature and marketing messaged graphics that showed how Crave supported its clients/customers. One of the "hottest" products, UFC Fightgame, was featured in a special Oriental room on the second level. The themed area included a zone where visitors could have their photos taken with a Champion UFC fighter or a UFC showgirl.

A majority of the walls and decks were rental structures to help overcome the budget constraints and the other elements of the exhibit were constructed of or trimmed with natural and corrugated metals, lumacite, fabric, wood and laminates, the Octanorm system and inflatable figures and forms.

FOX

CLIENT—*Fox Interactive*

TRADE SHOW—*E3, Los Angeles, CA*

DESIGNER—*Exhibitron, National City, CA*

DESIGN TEAM—*Viat Do/Joe Christiana*

FABRICATION—*Exhibitron*

SPACE—*5000 sq. ft.*

PHOTOGRAPHY—*Courtesy of Exhibitron*

The accent on Fox's 5000 sq. ft., dual-level exhibit at the E3 show was on Fox as the producer and deliverer of Entertainment for the entire family. Designed by Exhibitron, the exhibit consisted of seven different custom vignettes—each with its own design, ambiance and games to try. Whether it was a visit to a dark, dank, stony cave for Planet of the Apes or a moldy, gray crumbling Gothic ruin to partake in game playing with Buffy the Vampire Slayer, the ambiance was always amusing, enticing and somewhat inviting. Whether it

was a pile of skulls, gargoyles and tracery windows at the Buffy station where game players could pick up the challenge and try out the new game or at Sanity—a vignette filled with artifacts, games, superheroes and super-villains, the focus was on interaction. Faux painting, foam carving, dry ice and special effects and lighting made each stop a unique experience. In addition, "live" characters right out of the TV shows and the featured games strolled through the space interacting with the visitors and mimicking the action games in which they appear.

Directly over the cave setting for the Planet of the Apes and under the floating curved frames covered with a stretched, translucent fabric that carried the FOX name spelled out in huge yellow dimensional letters, was a 2500 sq.ft. deck which served as a refreshment area and also doubled as a place for seller-to-buyer conversing. Live entertainment took place on a small stage within the exhibit. The stage was backed up by a colorful, cutout of many characters from "The Simpsons"—a Fox network favorite. Since this was a completely open area, The Simpsons logo appeared overhead on a structo-grid and The Simpsons game could be viewed on flat plasma screens on either side of the raised platform.

FLOW

CLIENT—*Flow International Corp., Dick LeBlanc*

TRADE SHOW—*International Manufacturing Technology Show (IMTS) 2000, Chicago, IL*

DESIGNER—*Steelhead Productions, Poulsbo, WA*

DESIGN TEAM—*Scott Vance, lead designer*
  Roger Lyngclip, CAD

FABRICATION—*Steelhead Productions*

FABRICATION TEAM—*Scott McGraw/John Jorgensen*

LIGHTING—*Jim Andersen*

AUDIO-VISUALS—*McKnight Audio Visual*

SPACE—*5000 sq. ft.*

PHOTOGRAPHY—*Jamie Padgett & Co.*

The International Manufacturing Technology Show (IMTS) is held every second year at McCormick Place in Chicago. It is the largest tool and equipment buying show in North America and for eight days exhibitors and attendees can witness the latest marvels of machine technology usually presented in exhibits that seem to reflect "business-as-usual" images.

Flow International wanted something different for their 5000 sq. ft. space and wanted "to create a window within our exhibit strategy to make our leadership statement clear." Steelhead Productions created this revolutionary and unusual exhibit for Flow and Flow's gameplan which would "turn up the trade show marketing jets on their competition by raising the bar with the first really progressive exhibit design ever presented at IMTS."

"From the beginning of our design process we received creative license from Flow to stretch and develop." One of the challenges was to work around all the power cords, drain lines and feed lines required to energize the machines to be demonstrated during show hours. Steelhead designed a modular flooring system which was used in 50% of the booth. The aluminum diamond plate flooring was designed so that it could be configured to fit any portion of a 20 ft. x 20 ft. to 50 ft. x 100 ft. exhibit space. Also, live presenters used the floor as a stage to attract patrons to view the demonstrations. The platform was 8 in. above the cutting heads which enhanced the viewing of the performing machinery. Flow's equipment was positioned first in the exhibit space and then the floor was built around the massive pieces of machinery. "The raw concrete flooring system combined with the diamond plate flooring created a very deliberate 'industrial-look metaphor' and the carpeting was used in the registration and conference room areas."

The exhibit featured a central 24 ft. high mast assembly that impressively portrayed the corporate logo which was waterjet cut out of 1/2" aluminum plate. The mast assemblies were secured into the modular flooring system then rigged together with a series of tension wires. Theatrical lighting, installed throughout on the overhead truss, provided interesting reflectivity and product highlighting. Flow's corporate color is teal and all of the theatrical gels were teal so the space had an eerie glow in the

BENGAL® Waterjet Systems
World's Most Popular Waterjet
FlowMaster- Intelligent Software
FLOW
Waterjets

company's signature color. The overhead truss was also used to identify—graphically—the machines set beneath the appropriate graphic. The remaining floor space was developed into corporate identification towers which had raised, attached conference rooms.

The "progressive strategy" to energize the look and feel of Flow at the IMTS show paid off and Steelhead Productions developed a three year rental contract for the client.

LOUISIANA PACIFIC

CLIENT—*Louisiana Pacific International Home Builders*

TRADE SHOW—*International Builder's Show, Dallas, TX*

DESIGNER—*Derse Exhibits, Milwaukee, WI*

DESIGN TEAM—*Derek Dewberry / Michele Tarlo*

FABRICATION—*Derse Exhibits*

SPACE—*5000 sq. ft.*

PHOTOGRAPHY—*Jamie Padgett & Co.*

To fill the 5000 sq. ft. space that Louisiana Pacific took for the International Builder's Show in Dallas, Derse Exhibits was challenged to come up with a different look that "blended all of the different and expanding brands into one cohesive image." Louisiana Pacific is a multi-location building materials corporation that produces a wide variety of products for the residential builder/contractor/retail do-it-yourself and the industrial/OEM market. The goal was also to design "an environment that is visually educational, yet comfortable and inviting to attendees."

Most of the structures stood as high as 24 ft.—giving a very large presentation on the trade show floor. Since L-P's products are mostly angular and linear in nature, simple, straight structures were repeated throughout the exhibit. Soft, curved canopies were placed over the structures and the product display areas "to provide a calmer backdrop than the harsh look of the show hall ceiling." The canopies also helped to visually affect different environments for the larger product display zones. Actual product was integrated into the exhibit as design accents—ceiling joists were used for stability and facilitated lighting for the connecting towers.

The graphics used for the assorted brands were unified. 5 ft. x 9 ft. graphic panels that were created for each brand. One was placed alongside the aisle to provide general information about the adjacent product and a second graphic—for the same product and of the same size—with more detailed information, appeared within the interior of the exhibit—sometimes with actual products attached to the panels. Behind each graphic panel was a 14 ft. high supergraphic on fabric, "that conveyed the people of L-P and its customers."

"When you combine all the graphics, high logo identification, 14 ft. high fabric graphics, product graphic panels and literature into the exhibit, the attendee is educated at different levels as they approach and enter the L-P space and a very large three dimensional brand is created."

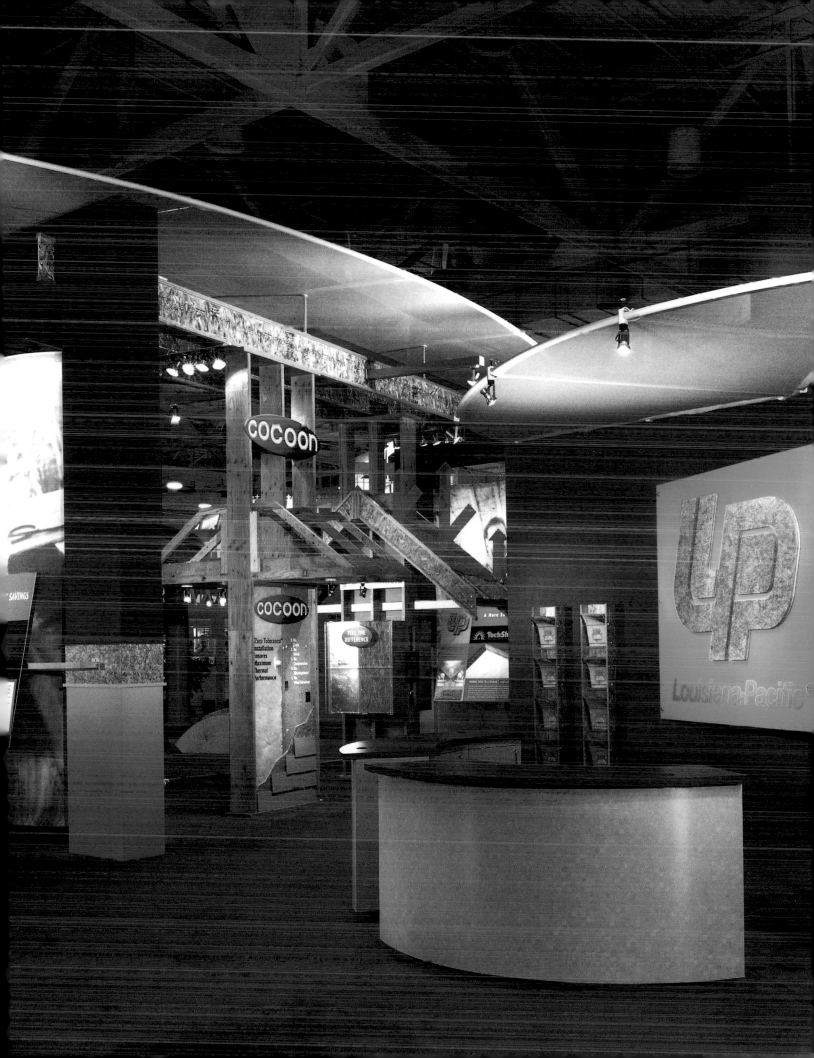

CISCO SYSTEMS

CLIENT—*Cisco Systems, Inc.*

TRADE SHOW—*Supercom 2000, Atlanta, GA*

DESIGNER—*Displayworks, Irvine, CA, Dave Jakel*

FABRICATION—*Displayworks*

SPACE—*5400 sq. ft.*

PHOTOGRAPHY—*Courtesy of Displayworks*

The 5400 sq. ft. exhibit was designed by Displayworks for Cisco System's appearance at the SuperCom show in Atlanta and it was a-swirl with curves, arcs and bends—almost like parts of a globe.

The high tech, 22nd Century look of the exhibit enhanced Cisco's image and its assorted space age products. The central, circular core structure was made up of metal bands rising up from the parquet flooring and the curved vertical bands arced over the many computers on display within its circumference. A series of circles—overhead—added to the globe-like look while also adding height and thus prominence for the total design.

Surrounding this core were curved architectural metal elements that on their upper parts carried giant graphics. These uprights created a circle around the core circle like images in space encircling the planet Earth represented by the "globe" in the middle. Bleacher type benches were integrated into some of these arched uprights for the live demonstrations that were performed on the open wood floor.

A dramatic, exciting and very enticing swirling staircase with maple wood steps floating in space and with a decorative handrail of maple and stainless steel led to an upper deck where private conference rooms were located—partially hidden from below by the previously mentioned graphics on fabric panels. Located beneath the deck was a large, curved bar with computers and monitors on top and space age stools in front so that attendees could get more "hands-on" information about what Cisco Systems had to offer.

Plasma screens, changing graphics, subdued lighting and the warmth of the maple wood panels and furniture juxtaposed with the steely metals and the eerie green glow of the machinery all created a most unique setting for Cisco Systems.

H P

CLIENT—*hp*

TRADE SHOW—*Network & Interop Show, Las Vegas, NV*

DESIGNER—*Landor Associates, San Francisco, CA*

DESIGN TEAM—*Jean Loo & Scott Drummond*

FABRICATION—*Contempo Designs*

FABRICATION TEAM—*Eric Harger/Jeff Johnson*

SPACE—*5600 sq. ft.*

PHOTOGRAPHY—*Courtesy of Landor Associates*

Based on the client's new identity, Landor Associates designed hp's new exhibit which appeared at the Network and Interop Show in Las Vegas. "Inspiration was taken from the elements of the core identity in the design of forms and the selection of materials."

The 5600 sq. ft. exhibit featured curved corners and shapes that reflected the softened shape of the idea unit. The frosted plexiglass, which played a major role in the look and finish of the exhibit, "resembled the white space vocabulary." Panels of the frosted plastic filled the aluminum grid that was used to construct the giant, curved corner tower of the exhibit. The upper part of this grid was an effective "screen" for the truly supergraphic images that were cast upon them. Another grid of brushed metal stood several feet in front of the actual structure and it carried large graphic panels in the uppermost openings of the grid. These were visible from almost any vantage point of the show. The graphics vocabulary which included the use of photography plus a select color palette and graphic icons were all integrated into the design of the exhibit to "establish a consistent voice for communicating the new hp invent brand."

Also, colored lights were integrated into the design to act and react on the areas of frosted plexiglass—especially when viewed from inside the exhibit. Workstations were set up along the plexi/grid wall and attendees could find out from hp's Open View what hp had to offer at this show.

A double staircase of lightweight metal treads and stainless rails led to the upper deck where conferencing took place. A presentation theater was also incorporated into the total design.

INTEL
CORP.

CLIENT—*Intel Corp,*

TRADE SHOW—*Siggraph '99, Atlanta, GA*

DESIGNER—*Mauk Designs, San Francisco, CA*

DESIGN TEAM—*Mitchell Mauk/Laurence Raines/Christiane Forstnig/James Pennington-Kent*

FABRICATION—*Exhibitgroup/Giltspur, SF, John Mastory*

SPACE—*5600 sq.ft.*

PHOTOGRAPHY—*Andy Caulfield, Needham Heights, MA*

The award winning, 5600 sq. ft. exhibit designed for Intel Corp. was a people-stopper at the Siggraph Show in Atlanta. As conceived and designed by Mauk Design, it not only made a strong impression for the new Pentium chip that was introduced but it "overwhelmed" all the senses while getting that message across.

The theme—"shorten the distance between thinking it and seeing it"—drove the exhibit's design language and forms. For the attendees at this show, speed is everything! Since most of the products were small in size (between 2 in. and 4 in.) something big had to hold them together and make the company's impression. What did it was the 20 ft. tall curved, metal-faced wall with wide openings that led into the actual exhibit space. Recessed in hundreds of self-illuminated, round shadow boxes that patterned the wall were the Pentium lll processors and other high performance products produced by Intel. The items were encased in clear, vacuum formed acrylic spheres. "Huge and encompassing, it remained light—floating 9 ft. off the ground."

Inside, the 40 ft. x 20 ft. theater was designed to reinforce the Intel message of speed to a continuous flow of people. The theater entrance portal was created out of five 52 in. flat screens and a brain image was printed on the scrim fabric that covered the screens. When the lights dimmed in front of the screens, renderings of robots—three feet behind the brain—appeared. "It was

TECHNOLOGY SHOWCASE

Evans & Sutherland
Lightning 1200

Cost effective 3D graphics solution
for MCAD & DCC customers

ATI
Rage Magnum

Rage 128, 32MB memory,
OpenGL® ICD, 2D / 3D entry
level solution

3Dlabs
Oxygen GCX

Maximum AutoCAD performance
using Permedia2 graphics
processor with Soft Engine 4

NEO
166E

Fast OpenGL® performance for
high end CAD/CG
Custom LSI for
geometry/rendering

Evans & Sutherland
AccelGalaxy

Powerhouse for 3D animation and
visual simulation applications

Tridium Research
DG4-AG3

Widescreen DVD, 3D,
Direct Draw across dual monitors
without interference

3Dlabs
Oxygen GVX1

Heavy-duty,
geometry-accelerated
workstation graphics for
below $1,000

a fantastic, eye-catching trick that tied into Intel's ad campaign and marketing thrust." While waiting to get into the theater, attendees were entertained with splash screens on a series of flat panel monitors. To cut down the feeling of waiting on a long line, five queues were organized instead of one. All of the exterior walls of the theater were made of 5mm thick Sintra, jet cut into typography that spelled out Intel's show theme. Behind that screen of cutout letters were flat plasma monitors which replayed the inside audience's reactions to the passersby outside the enclosure.

Adding to the color, excitement and entertainment of the Intel exhibit were the colored gobos and the backlit demonstration counters where colorful images glowed. "Lighting created an aura of excitement" and that excitement carried through the entire space.

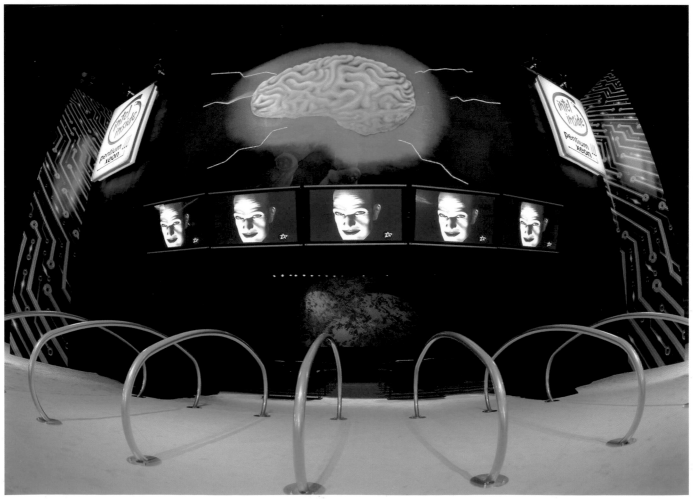

RAINBOW MEDIA

CLIENT—*Rainbow Media*

TRADE SHOW—*National Cable Television Assoc. (NCTA),*
New Orleans, LA

DESIGNER—*Mauk Design, San Francisco, CA*

DESIGN TEAM—*Mitchell Mauk / Adam Brodsley*
Christiane Forstnig

FABRICATION—*Premier Displays, Frederique Georges*

SPACE—*5600 sq. ft.*

PHOTOGRAPHY—*Andy Caulfield, Needham Heights, MA*

For the sake of making a stronger impact at the National Cable Television Association's show, Rainbow Media, which consists of five cable TV channels, changed from five individual exhibits to a single, consolidated exhibit with five distinct personalities.

The overall "umbrella" was designed by Mauk Design and each brand was anchored in a 15 ft. disk at the foot of the aluminum tube arches. In the center of the exhibit was a rotating bar set against a kidney shaped conference room structure. The AMC area had a simplified Hollywood deco look that tied in with the channel's movie lineup. Rich wood paneling, terrazzo tiles and the patterned deco furniture created a relaxed seating area. Romance Classics, which is targeted at female viewers, had a sitting area filled with a palette of bright, feminine colors and contemporary styled furniture. Other areas

VIEWERS CONNECT WITH RAINBOW

such as Bravo, Much Music and the Independent Film Channel were also appropriately set to suit the subject matter from black, chrome and polished granite tiled floors for the high-end, cultural Bravo, to the raw and rough feel of fiberboard and recycled tire tread flooring for the Independent Film Channel.

Circling over the brushed metal circular bar were five indentifying brand logos connected by the cutout Rainbow logo. Of special interest was the "Viewers Connect with Rainbow" wall which showed the company's sense of community with its viewers. The wall was covered with e-mail messages, faxes and letters written by the viewers and "it was fascinating to see jaded trade show attendees stopping, reading and at times smiling at the comments."

SONY

CLIENT—*Sony Electronics*

TRADE SHOW—*Comdex, Las Vegas, NV*

DESIGNER—*Thinc Design, New York, NY*

DESIGN TEAM—*Tom Hennes/Janet Cross/Mike Graziolo/Glen Rossman*

FABRICATION—*Structural Display, Long Island City, NY, Paul Palazzo*

SPACE—*6000 sq. ft.*

PHOTOGRAPHY—*Courtesy of Thinc Design*

Sony had not previously had a major presence at Comdex—The International Computer Show—but now they wanted to "dominate the show floor with a presence that would strikingly emphasize their strategy by redefining the consumer's relationship with the computer." The design, created by Thinc Design, not only had to reposition Sony's image in this 6000 sq. ft. space but simultaneously raised the level of presentation at Comdex. " To give an impression of the richness of experience that convergence promised, we developed a highly theatrical environ-

ment of playful shapes and moving lifestyle images, utilizing rich color and unconventional video presentations."

The circular theater, topped with a glowing dome, dominated the booth. The dome was a concentric pair of stretched fabric structures; the interior layer was cotton theatrical scrim to optimize the soft lighting and the outer layer was an opaque tent fabric which appeared solid. Using an innovative, self-contained sprinkler system, the designers were permitted to install 164 seats in the theater. "Trackball interfaces were created in fiberglass, metals and acrylics and scrim ceilings provided diaphanous projection surfaces. The theater screen and projector movements were fully automated and the graphic images and type were projected in moving multicolored light, or in cascading video images which traveled from one monitor to another."

In other areas of the exhibit, Sony's concept of the total integration of computing, communication and entertainment technology was presented in a home environment "styled and accessorized to be more visionary than realistic." Conference rooms were also provided as well as a "Shooting Gallery" where visitors could test Sony's new digital still cameras.

32 interactive network stations enabled visitors to experience—hands on—access to information. The open plan of the exhibit allowed an easy flow through the space and also encouraged guests to sample, try and experience all that Sony had to offer.

GLIMCHER

CLIENT—*Glimcher Realty Trust*

TRADE SHOW—*ISCS, Lass Vegas, NV*

DESIGNER—*Tony L Horton Design, Houston, TX*

DESIGN TEAM—*Tony L. Horton: president*
  Gus Hamsho and Krystyna Bojanowski: Architects
  Mike Van Pamel: Graphic Director.

FABRICATION—*Tony L Horton Design*

VP PRODUCTION—*Wayne Keown*

SPACE—*6237 sq. ft.*

PHOTOGRAPHY—*Aker/Zvonkovic Photography*

The International Shopping Center Show is where shopping center/mall developers and realtors go to show off who they are, what they have accomplished and show attendees who they should be interested in teaming up with. Glimcher Realty Trust took the opportunity in their 6237 sq.ft. exhibit, designed by Tony L Horton, to present their accomplishments with style and panache.

Located in a corner of the convention center, it was a challenge to drive traffic to the exhibit. The very tall ID tower that grew up from its surrounding inner colonnade together with the custom arched light sconces managed to attract attention from across the vast hall to the Glimcher exhibit and, consequently, drew crowds. The tower, gleaming in brushed aluminum and hard rock maple laminate made an elegant plinth and it carried the

Glimcher name on top. The custom light sconces threw a tremendous amount of white light into the exhibit as well as help to create a traffic flow pattern inside the exhibit space.

A stylized, elegant colonnade formed around the tower and at the base served as an area for quiet conferencing. Standing almost in front of it was the brushed aluminum curved reception desk. The floor of the exhibit area was maple wood patterned every 4 ft. with a 1/2 in. strip of stainless steel. The roller coated outer walls, the custom carpeting and the leather chairs also added a sense of "permanence" to what was really a temporary exhibit.

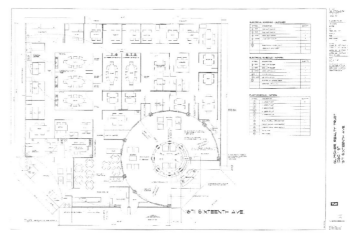

To sell their product, the Glimcher properties were treated as "art pieces" and photos or renderings were beautifully framed and hung on the curved, semicircular wall that served as the perimeter of the exhibit. Like the rest of the subtle, sophisticated and up-scaled look of the exhibit, it carried through the art gallery theme proposed by the designers. The use of natural, neutral materials such as wood, leather and steel created a "comfortable yet elegant environment in which the client could conduct business."

MACERICH CO.

CLIENT—*The Macerich Co.*

TRADE SHOW—*ISCS, Las Vegas, NV*

DESIGNER—*T L Horton Design, Houston, TX*

DESIGN TEAM—*Tony L. Horton: President
    Steven Levesque: Designer, Paul Hicks*

FABRICATION—*T L Horton Design*

FABRICATION TEAM—*Wayne Keown, VP Production*

SPACE—*6300 sq. ft.*

PHOTOGRAPHY—*Zvonkovic Photography*

The 110 linear feet of frontage for the 6300 sq. ft. space at the ISCS 2000 show created a challenge for the T L Horton Design group. To solve it the designers of the Macerich Co. booth created an architectural tower, 16 ft. high, made of maple veneer and stainless steel with frosted glass panels that glowed from within. Stretched across the very top lintel was the client's name in three dimensional letters. Sitting directly in front of the dramatic portal was the semicircular reception desk sheathed in maple veneer. The space beyond the tower was divided into assorted areas of interest by the use of the three shaped walls made of different materials.

Maple veneers and stained maple panels defined the "gallery" area and a hard rock maple, solid wood floor

was used to highlight this zone. Set out on the undulating, free form wood wall were photos of The Macerich Co. properties. On the wood floor were clusters of soft, easy chairs arranged for easy one-on-one conversations or just a quiet moment of rest.

The giant, 17 ft. high bronze metal map became a "wall" and the aluminum details highlighted the client's national strength. Several, freestanding kiosks served to feature other Macerich projects in work and the kiosks could be viewed from all directions. Food service was provided at this end of the exhibit space on the light looking wood and metal furniture. This was the café/meeting area as opposed to the map/locations area previously mentioned.

The net result of the exhibit's design, the creative use of the space and the natural materials used was to help "transform the client's image to one of strength and sophistication."

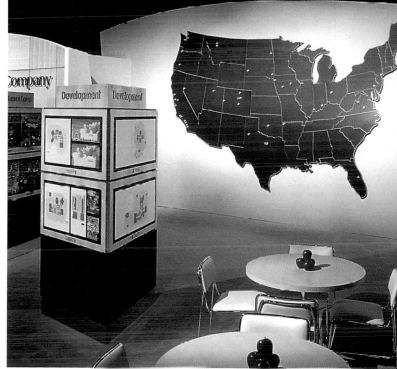

SEAGATE

CLIENT—*Seagate Technology, Inc.*

TRADE SHOW—*Comdex, Las Vegas, NV*

DESIGNER—*Thinc Design, New York, NY*

DESIGN TEAM—*Tom Hennes/Rich Stockton Dana Christensen/Marna Clark*

FABRICATION—*Exhibitree*

LIGHTING DESIGN—*Paul Palazzo*

SPACE—*6563 sq. ft.*

PHOTOGRAPHY—*Courtesy of Thinc Design*

Thinc Design, the designers of the 6563 sq.ft. exhibit for Seagate Technology, Inc. at the Comdex show boasted of the fact that not a single inch of plastic laminate was used in the entire display. Seagate had recently initiated a strategy of hardware/software intelligence storage that was especially beneficial for larger enterprises—and this was a shift from their hardware focused commodity business of building hard drives. The new strategy also proposed a new way of looking at storage and that inspired Thinc's tag line—"See Storage Differently."

information the way you want it

enterprise information management

storage networking

The exhibit had to capture and capitalize on widespread exposure because this was "an industry wide call-to-arms." The exhibit's design included a 50 ft. wide, "drive-in" theater that was visible to much of the show floor. The wide screen, high definition video, shot in 2-D, also utilized a 3-D overlay of laser graphics. Custom glasses, in the shape of Seagate's logo, were first used to remove a layer of confusing "data" from the information at the film's beginning and later were unfolded to process the 3-D effect of the program. The glasses, attached to lanyards and worn around the neck, were later seen on attendees walking around the show floor and thus they served as invitations to others to check out Seagate's exhibit.

The exhibit also included live technology demonstrations and there were technology-enabled information desks located in the space. An acoustically insulated but visually permeable conference room was also included. "All the components of the exhibit, from the lenticular graphics that changed as attendees walked by them, to the see-through graphics which covered the conference room, were tied in some way to the 'See Storage Differently' theme."

FITEL
TECHNOLOGY

CLIENT—*Fitel Technology, Inc.*

TRADE SHOW—*Optical Fiber Communications Conference, Anaheim, CA.*

DESIGNER—*MC2, Jeff Serivatien*

DESIGN TEAM—*Rob Murphy*

FABRICATION—*MC2, Pen Argyl, PA*

LIGHTING—*LightSpeed*

SPACE—*6800 sq. ft.*

PHOTOGRAPHY—*Jamie Padgett & Co.*

What made the Fitel Technology's 6800 sq.ft. exhibit at the Optical Fiber Communications Conference so unique was that the exhibit kept changing color. As designed by MC2, the central motif was a technical formula demonstrating how Fitel's components combined to make a system. This motif was used as a backdrop/setting/wallpaper/stripping throughout the space.

60 X 80 Booth

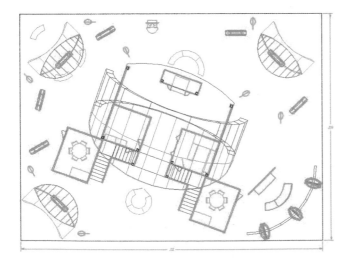

The space was broken up into individual areas of interest by wire framed, stretched fabric canopies that served to highlight the unusual teardrop shaped fixtures, standing on the floor, that showcased some of Fitel's new products. Sweeping overhead, above the major two level high structure, was an even higher flying canopy that—like the Jefferson Memorial in St. Louis—created a framework for the client's giant brand logo. The double decker structure invited attendees to enter and "Discover the Next Dimension in Optical Communications." The semicircular stainless reception desk stood directly in front. Inside there were demonstration areas, hands-on stations, educational information presented with graphics on TV monitors and products displayed in curved showcases. Throughout, the large rectangular space yielded to curves and arced elements.

The client's marketing strategy served as a common backdrop for all of the graphic presentations—both static and AV. These campaigns, product positioning and technical sales information were blended "to produce a cohesive brand experience." What Fitel hoped to accomplish and what was made apparent to the attendees was that Fitel was more than a name of component parts but a corporate leader of complete systems.

What made this open, free-to-move-about exhibit so attention getting and riveting was the use of the gobos that moved, danced and hopped from surface to surface and changed the fabric covered canopies from red to pink to purple to blue and teal.

CISCO SYSTEMS

CLIENT—*Cisco Systems, Inc.*

TRADE SHOW—*Networld + Interop 2000, Atlanta, GA*

DESIGNER—*Mauk Design, San Francisco, CA*

DESIGN TEAM—*Mitchell Mauk/Laurence Raines/
Gary Helfand/James Pennington-Kent*

FABRICATION—*Displayworks, Mark Hubbell/Anthony
Mendoza*

SPACE—*7000 sq. ft.*

PHOTOGRAPHY—*Andy Caulfield, Needham Heights, MA*

The 70 ft. x 100 ft. exhibit by Mauk Design was created as a "three dimensional expression of Cisco's corporate values and graphic standards" and it was introduced at the Networld + Interop 2000 Show in Atlanta. The challenge was to establish a consistent image using Cisco's corporate ID and brand identity and also address the fact that the Cisco exhibit may be used in other shows in spaces that may vary from 40 ft. x 40 ft. to 100 ft. x 100 ft. islands. The program had to be adaptable and there was also a need for quick change of graphics and still maintain an open and inviting environment that allowed for the redressing with graphics and messages and still be cost effective.

Large cylinders and gently curved walls were used to announce Cisco's "stability." The new design made use of a raised floor in the center "as a central nervous system spine." The modular floor was designed to expand or contract in 2 ft. increments to fit a wide range of possible floor plans while using the same size components. Sitting atop this warm, cork covered computer floor were racks of technolo-

gy and user-friendly, hands-on demos of the client's products which were set out on softly glowing glass tabletops. The demo stations had roll around, metal laminate doors and recessed aluminum keyboard trays while the supporting aluminum feet wore red rubber bumper pads. Product displays were shown on plasma screens which could be rolled into position along the wall on red, in-line, skate wheels.

The all-important theater consisted of the two towers which were constructed with matte aluminum mullions

Empowering the Internet Generation

filled with lenticular iridescent blue panels. The big screen—like a gigantic TV monitor—was wedged between the towers. The semi walls with wide openings to either side, were finished with a metallic fiber wallpaper in a warm, graphite color and they were decorated, three dimensionally, with the Benday dot pattern which is part of Cisco's ID standards. That same pattern appeared on the illuminated light-box panels and on the translucent plastic area signs. The benches in the theater

were inflated tube cushions on a marine plywood base and, like the demo tables, the aluminum feet were finished with Cisco red rubber bumper pads.

"The appearance of this exhibit focused on a message of stability, reliability and humanity (the many faces that appear in the graphics) in an industry known for none of these things. Because the product had no outward signs with which to evaluate these attributes, the product took on the qualities of the environment."

CISCO SYSTEMS

CLIENT—*Cisco Systems, Inc.*

TRADE SHOW—*Networld + Interop 2000, Las Vegas, NV*

DESIGNER—*Displayworks, Irvine, CA*

FABRICATION—*Displayworks*

SPACE—*7150 sq. ft.*

PHOTOGRAPHY—*Courtesy of Displayworks*

The subtle metallic skin that covered the architectural constructions in the Cisco Systems' 7150 sq.ft. space at the Networld + Interop Show 2000, cast a silvery sheen over the entire space. Displayworks designed two gigantic, towering, multistory high structures connected by a walkway and an open mezzanine high off the show floor. The circular tower, at one end, is like a silo and the metal pipe construction created a grid which was filled in with frosted lucite panels on the upper levels while the lower ones were clear lucite and showed off the Cisco systems at work. The other structure—like a colon— was an arced unit with angular extensions coming out of it. These pro-

jections repeated the frosted lucite grid that appeared on the cylindrical tower. At ground level there were six hands-on demonstration stations where attendees could get in and find out more about Cisco Systems.

Taking their cue from the Cisco Systems logo, bright red appears throughout as an accent note. There is the towering red pyramid that ended by piercing the flat red roof that extended off one of the structures. Red carpeting was used as part of the show floor to bring the attendees to the curved, sweeping open metal staircase with metal pipe railings that led up to the mezzanine level where refreshments were served and conferring space was available.

A semicircular amphitheater was integrated into the design with a half round stage. The red upholstered raised arcs served as backrests in lieu of seats for the standing viewers. It made getting people in and out more efficient—and faster. Throughout, graphics were used to add color, warmth and to restate the "empowering" concept of Cisco Systems. Some photos were many stories high while others were four or five feet in diameter. Changing graphics and images, produced on the flat screens, added to the excitement in the otherwise elegant, architectural setting. Cisco Systems' red brand logos—brilliantly backlit—were applied to the tops of the structures so that they could be seen from anywhere on the show floor.

IOMEGA

CLIENT—*Iomega*

TRADE SHOW—*Comdex 2000, Las Vegas, NV*

DESIGNER—*MC2, Las Vegas, NV*

DESIGN TEAM—*Jeff Cameron/Todd Sussman/Kahori Sako*

FABRICATION—*MC2, Las Vegas, NV & Pen Argyl, PA*

FABRICATION TEAM—*Beth Kazelskis/Steve Clark/*
Jeff Zukowski/Sam Salde Briwn White/Vince Cozza/
Bob McNulty

LIGHT & AUDIO VISUALS—*MC2 & Cornerstone*

SPACE—*7200 sq. ft.*

PHOTOGRAPHY—*Jamie Padgett & Co.*

This exhibit, designed by MC2 for Iomega, was a key
component in the firm's rebranding campaign. It was
revealed at the Comdex 2000 show and the design
expanded and transferred the popularity and reputation
of Iomega's Zip Drive to the new line of computer
peripheral products. The exhibit also projected "a hip,
fun image attractive to Generation X-types."

The exhibit's plan is circular in design and fills the
7200 sq.ft. space with curves. Attendees begin their
"tour" at the streamlined, arced registration desk then
move on to the semicircular theater after passing by a
plasma wall that provides a degree of privacy for the
demonstration area. From there, the visitors are drawn
into one of the three galleries; one straight ahead and the
others to the right and the left.

The round, central gallery had a sail cloth ceiling "covered with dancing points of projected light." The client's
products were displayed on clear oval disks surrounded
by clear plastic halos and the fixtures were supported on
sleek, silver-toned legs. "Product design details were
incorporated into the exhibit design" such as the blue
oval sconces which were mounted on the center column.

They were reminiscent of the Zip 250 Hard Drive. The red swirl pattern in the carpet recalled the red swirl motion indicator of the Predator CDRW.

Attendees were free to move about in this museum-like curved corridor. The Iogema "i" was used as the support structure of the handrail around the plastic floor panels. Demonstration areas were also located within this inner circle. In the outer semicircular structure that complemented the theater, on the opposite side several assorted size conference rooms were found. A pair of staircases on the outer perimeter led to the upper deck of this structure.

"One-to-one product demonstrations were designed to be ergonomically and design appropriate for the products." The demo station for the Hip Zip MP3 audio player, as an example, was designed with the same "fits well in your hand" curve as the product and sideless and backless stools made visitors just comfortable enough to try the product without enticing them to stay longer than necessary.

The display won several BMA awards at this show.

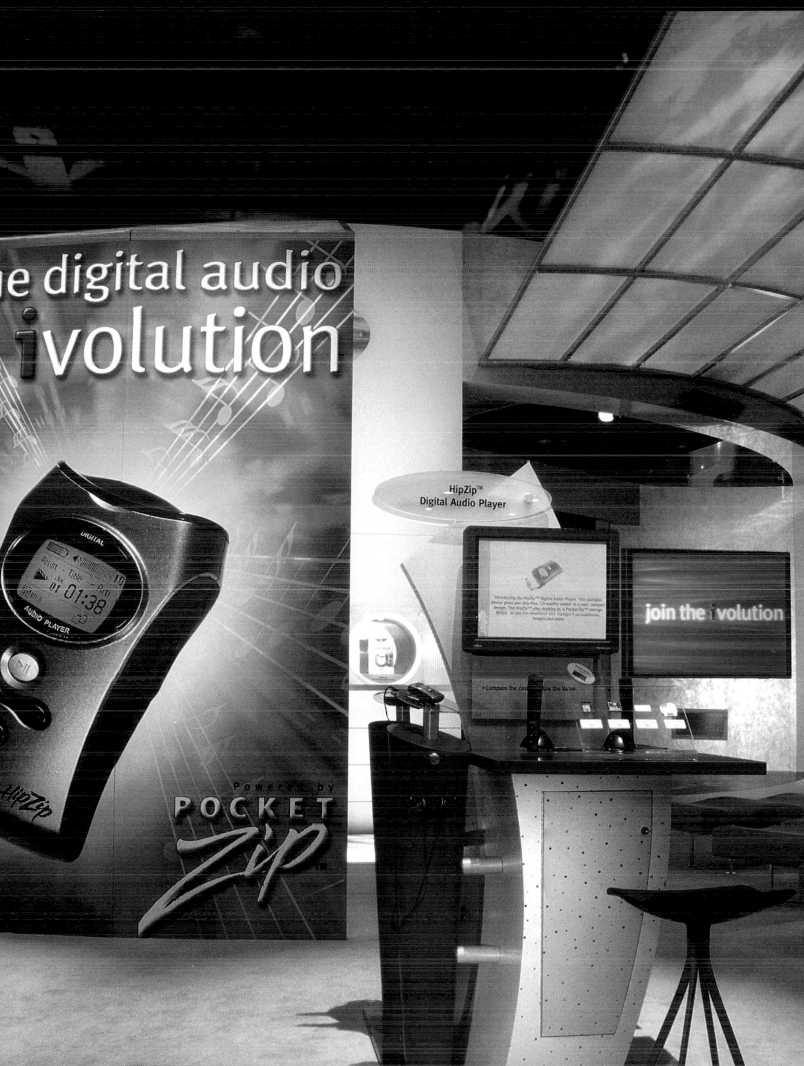

DISNEY
INTERACTIVE

CLIENT—*Disney Interactive*

TRADE SHOW—*E3, Los Angeles, CA*

DESIGNER—*Exhibitgroup/Giltspur, NY*

DESIGN TEAM—*Alex Kaluzschner/Daniel Maldonado/*
  Nick Bragin

FABRICATION—*Exhibitgroup/Giltspur, NY*

FABRICATION TEAM—*Mark Swan/Linda Zitelli/*
  Brian Schiels/John O'Neil

LIGHTING AND AV—*Intelecon*

SPACE—*8000 sq. ft.*

PHOTOGRAPHY—*Jamie Padgett & Co.*

Disney is always a recognizable name at any trade show and the company's purpose for taking an 8000 sq.ft. space and having this exhibit designed for them by the New York division of Exhibitgroup/Giltspur was to further reinforce their position as "a leading developer, marketer and distributor of high quality, award winning interactive entertainment and educational CD Roms and video games."

The challenge for the design firm was to "maintain the Disney look and feel" while showing off a wide variety of titles—from "Who Wants to be a Millionaire?" to the "Magic Artists" series. The floor plan "separated business from pleasure." For the attendees doing the show, the big "pleasure" attraction was the "Mickey" kiosks where games were demonstrated and the many other Disney character-related graphics boldly and colorfully added to the fun feeling of the space. The "Mickey" kiosks were grouped according to game classifications with four, five, or six units making a pod. The five demo pod clusters featured "Creativity," "Learning," and game titles, while the six demo pod starred "Junior Games." Each demo unit looked like a super-toy construction with bulbous yellow plastic bases, red seats to

straddle and angular, perforated uprights that supported the angled monitors. These three pod clusters were located up front—off the aisle—to catch the interest of the show visitors. Also up front, in one corner, was a "game arcade" in which 12 demo units were lined up. The tunnel-like arcade feeling was reinforced by the semi open canopy over that space.

The exhibit seemed to have been anchored by an inverted, truncated cone of stretched fabric glowing with a cool light. It served to separate the curved blue reception desk from the dimly lit café just beyond which carried brilliant Disney character graphics on TV monitors

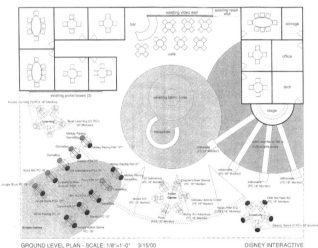

GROUND LEVEL PLAN - SCALE: 1/8"=1'-0"   3/15/00   DISNEY INTERACTIVE

which showcased some of the products. A recreation of the "Millionaire" stage set—even to the "hot seat"—was included in the exhibit and here a continually-hosted contest was conducted during show hours.

For the "business" end of the exhibit, conference rooms, offices and storage were set away from the heavily trafficked demonstration areas. That helped to keep the background noise to a minimum especially in the conference areas.

LEVI'S MOTHERSHIP

CLIENT—*Levi Straus & Co. and Foote, Cone & Belding*

TRADE SHOW—*Magic, Las Vegas, NV*

DESIGN—*Mauk Design, San Francisco, CA*

DESIGN TEAM—*Mitchell Mauk/Adam Brodsley/
    James Pennington-Kent*

FABRICATION—*Pinnacle Exhibits*

FABRICATION TEAM—*Chris Olberding & Bob Roth*

SPACE—*9000 sq. ft.*

PHOTOGRAPHY—*Any Caulfield, Needham Heights, MA*

Levi Straus & Co.'s prime objective at the Magic Menswear show was to position itself as "leaders in men's apparel trends." For several years they had been perceived as "followers" rather than "leaders" and this new exhibit, designed by Mauk Design for the 9000 sq.ft. space, attempted and succeeded in changing the company's look. "The client was acutely aware that a massive 'corporate' exhibit would alienate buyers focused on unique, individual style." According to Mitchell Mauk, the designer, "It had to be all things for all brands so we designed it as a village with a variety of elements set in a loose visual framework."

The conference rooms—18 in all—recalled "caves" that might have been carved out of mountains and their glass windows all faced towards a central piazza. "Each of the upper conference rooms was canted at a random

angle to break up the unfriendly monolithic wall so prevalent at Magic." The garments were displayed in a few very focused showcases. From the piazza, attendees could view each room's contents. More fashions were presented on the 18 ft. high towers —"allowing the clothing to be the hero."

The actual design concept is a modular one and there were two "room" sizes; 10 ft. x10 ft. and 20 ft. x 20 ft. Rails at the top and bottom walls were installed to accommodate 3 ft. x 10 ft. wall panels which could easily be changed for future reuses. Each "brand" had its own material vocabulary and by the selection of color or material for the inset panels the rooms were specialized and easily distinguished.. Levi's was recognized by the blue ridged aluminum, German white dot pattern on the curved desk and partition wall and the translucent red

plexiglas. Dockers was delineated by the use of stainless steel while Slates was represented by a cream colored concrete board. A second story flooring system was used along with non-slip, oil-refinery steps.

This award winning exhibit was cited for "its combination of broad yet finite, approachable yet exclusive, elegant yet human character and design and its success in implementing the Levi's brand."

VANITY FAIR

CLIENT—*Vanity Fair Corp.*

TRADE SHOW—*Magic, Menswear, Las Vegas, NV*

DESIGNER—*Exhibitgroup/Giltspur, Portland*

SUSAN MOSSCROP—*Creative Director*

FABRICATION—*Exhibitgroup Giltspur, Portland*

DAVID HANCOCK—*Director of Operations*

SPACE—*9900 sq. ft.*

PHOTOGRAPHY—*Jamie Padgett & Co.*

Since Vanity Fair Corporation had eight brand names to present at the Magic Menswear show, the designers, Exhibitgroup/Giltspur of Portland, selected a European town piazza as their design metaphor. In this way they were able to individually feature and visually present each of the client's brands in the 9900 sq. ft. space.

The curved, welcoming portal entrance to the exhibit area featured, on one side, a wall of TV monitors that provided a preview of "things to come." The other side presented the logos of the brands collected under the VF logo which appeared over the entrance. Visitors were invited to move through a display arcade with display

windows, and giant brand graphics lining the two sides. Overhead, a series of high-flying light bridges provided the sparkling light that illuminated the displayed garments and the wood laid floor.

Within the space, using assorted materials and colors, the designers created a collection of "boutiques" which represented and presented the newest products of each brand. A circular, raised "gazebo"—very high-tech and streamlined—centered the piazza and the boutiques encircled this element. The gazebo provided some seating, and though open and exposed, allowed visitors to "withdraw" from the traffic without. The steely look of the centerpiece was warmed by the illuminated brand signage above and the polka dot pattern of VF logos.

The show windows surrounding the Piazza as well as the featured fully illuminated display windows set into the perimeter walls of the exhibit, that were viewed by the attendees walking the aisles around the exhibit, were effectively merchandised and illuminated. The garments were shown as they might appear in an upscale, display-conscious, retail store.

CHRYSLER MOTORS

PRODUCT—*Chrysler / Jeep*

CLIENT—*Chrysler Motors*

TRADE SHOW—*Paris Motorshow*

DESIGN & FABRICATION—*The George P. Johnson Co., Auburn Hills, MI*

DESIGNER—*Paul Hemsworth*

SPACE—*12,480 sq. ft.*

PHOTOGRAPHY—*Paul Hemsworth*

To launch the new Sebring Cabriolet, the PT Cruiser and also celebrate the 60th anniversary and the special edition Jeep line, this 12,480 sq. ft. exhibit was designed by the George P. Johnson Co. for Chrysler Motors. Not only was this spectacular designed to appeal to and impress the European press, it was also hoped that it would build awareness for the Chrysler and Jeep brands with the thousands of visitors who would fill the Paris Motorshow.

According to the designers, the challenge was born out of the space and its location. The 25 meter wide and 48 meter deep area was bordered by an escalator along an entire front of the space which "completely obstructed visibility and access." Another problem was the sizable structure in the Mercedes-Benz exhibit space—on the other side of the aisle—that prevented any easy look into the Jeep stand. There were also three building columns along the aisle side of which the forward one became the narrow entry into the space.

Faced with these logistical problems, the designers came up with this dramatic setting composed of a series of circular wooden platforms—raised up one, two, three and four steps—set into the blue carpeted floor and the matching wood faced vertical pylons that carry the Jeep name. All around the space swaths of signature blue curved wire-framed fabric panels created a swirling and animated setting for the assorted vehicles and they were balanced by the large framed vertical panels that carried the Chrysler logo. The non-directional flow of the "traffic" added to the sense of movement and excitement in the exhibit space while still maintaining a feeling of class and brand name integrity. Individual kiosks, set out on the circular platforms along with the autos, graphically provided information about the featured models.

CHRYSLER

PT CRUISER

PONTIAC

CLIENT—*General Motors / Pontiac / GMC*

TRADE SHOW—*North American International Auto Show (NAIAS), Detroit, MI*

DESIGNER—*Exhibitgroup / Giltspur, Chicago, IL*

FABRICATION—*Exhibitgroup / Giltspur, Chicago*

SPACE—*20,000 sq. ft.*

PHOTOGRAPHY—*Jamie Padgett & Co.*

One of the dramatic elements of this 20,000 sq. ft. exhibit designed by the Chicago division of Exhibit-group/Giltspur for the Pontiac division of General Motors was the upper deck structure—an element previously not seen at an NAIAS show. The exhibit design accomplished what it had to do; it created an "extreme branding opportunity for Pontiac."

The architectural design and the graphic elements that were used "echoed Pontiac's bold, athletic brand character" and then supported that image and emphasized its attributes through the unique interactive experiences pro-

vided on the show floor. The strong metallic structural look of the exhibit and the very dramatic, high-tech metal grid ceiling along with the aforementioned deck all were complemented by the multicolored, floor-to-ceiling, finlike banners in a rainbow of colors. Each banner featured a different Pontiac product. Crisscrossing over the vast expanse of the trade show exhibit space were Pontiac's newest autos. Some were presented flat on the floor while others were tipped, angled or set askew to create a sense of movement and excitement—two major characteristics of the product. Huge, odd shaped, fabric covered forms created semi-dividing walls on the floor;

157

creating traffic patterns that assured the attendee of seeing everything. These were covered with full color, animated graphics that like the diagonally angled panels, added to that feeling of fun—of freedom—of movement.

The designers credited the extensive use of stretched fabric graphics and the "oversized intense colored billboard graphics" for adding an extra dimension in delivering the client's message.

KODAK FILM & CONSUMER IMAGING PRODUCTS

CLIENT—*Eastman Kodak*

TRADE SHOW—*Pavilion, Atlanta Olympic Game, Atlanta, GA*

DESIGN—*Exhibit Group/Giltspur, Rochester, NY*

DESIGN TEAM—*Tim Prinzing, Creative Director*

FABRICATOR—*Exhibit Group/Giltspur, Rochester, NY*

FABRICATION TEAM—*Jim Miller, Operations Manager*

LIGHT & AUDIO DESIGN—*Go Media Productions!!!*

SPECIAL PROPS—*Exhibit Group/Giltspur, Rochester, NY*

SPACE—*20,000 sq. ft.*

PHOTOGRAPHER—*Jamie Padgett & Co.*

The theme—"Take Pictures Further"—not only inspired the exhibit designers to take their design concept to the outer limits but also opened up myriad opportunities for having fun and giving fun in this 20,000 sq. ft. spectacular exhibit created by Exhibit Group/Giltspur for Kodak.

The location, the Pavilion at the Atlanta Summer Olympic Games in Atlanta, GA provided the occasion to invite the public in and have them experience the Kodak Experience. The opening statement—"World of Imaging"—also introduced the giant roll of film that started under the signature yellow Kodak name and would continue to unreel within. Bright, sharp primary colors dominated in the blacked out space and the giant scale undulating roll of film continued overhead and served to lead visitors from one interactive area to the next.

At the assorted stations visitors were invited to move, manipulate, press and/or print out all sorts of "how-tos." In addition to the saturated festival colors there were the super sized and super fun graphics. Also introduced here was the digital printing which was new at that time. "On this Global stage Kodak sang for the world to hear and see that digital printing works." Many of the design concepts depicted digitally enlarged Olympic moments like high diving from Boulder Dam.

SONY PLAYSTATION

CLIENT—*Sony Electronic Entertainment*

TRADE SHOW—*E3, '97, Atlanta, GA*

DESIGNER—*Thinc Design, NY*

DESIGN TEAM—*Tom Hennes/Victor D'Alessio/Sasha Marbury/Mike Graziolo/Donald Maldonado/Dusan Mosscrop/Steven Cook*

FABRICATION—*Exhibitgroup/Giltspur Chris Olberding*

LIGHTING—*Paul Palazzo*

AUDIO VISUAL—*Clarity*

SPACE—*37,000 sq. ft.*

PHOTOGRAPHY—*Courtesy of Thinc Design*

A significant part of the exhibit designed by Thinc Design for Sony PlayStation was directed towards game developers—many of whom are independents—and their choice of a given platform (PlayStation, Nintendo, Sega, etc.) often determines much of the initial revenue flow for that game. Since PlayStation may at any one time have 500 games to offer, the 37,000 sq. ft. exhibit at the E3 show in Atlanta also had to attract buyers, consumers—and the press.

"The primary challenge was to build an active, branded, coherent space in this fragmented, competitive environment." To accomplish this the designers created connections through the space via an elevated walkway system on which multiple large scale, tunnel-like electronic elements—called Boosters—literally surrounded visitors with TV monitors and images. These Boosters acted in unison with the centrally located, two-level, hexagonal shaped theater—The Primordium. Thus, the frequent

events that took place in this "center of the gaming universe" and other parts of the exhibit area could be seen in these Boosters anywhere in the exhibit space. The Primordium "used an interplay between a large revolving octahedron at its center with game images projected onto it from the multiple sides and five large peripheral flat projection screens." The programs that were presented showed the origin of the games and this imagery was projected and reviewed periodically throughout the space, namely in the Boosters on the elevated walkways.

In addition, there was a large café area as well as a conference center. In several locations there were semi-dark, "game arcades" where consumers could step up and personally experience the new Sony PlayStation titles. As

through most of the low lit exhibit area, light gobos were used and stars of assorted designs floated, skipped and jumped from one deep blue surface to the next. Some special areas of the exhibit were themed to suit the kind of games offered. An excellent example was the Adventure area which looked like something out of Raiders of the Lost Ark combined with African totems and a cave-like ambiance. Here, too, the gobos added a special light and dark play to the mood-inducing environment.

Remarkably, the entire project was conceived and executed in a 12 week time frame.

SONY PLAYSTATION

CLIENT—*Sony Computer Enterprises of America*

SHOW—*E3, Atlanta, GA*

DESIGNER—*Mauk Designs, San Francisco, CA*

DESIGN TEAM—*Mitchell Mauk/Adam Brodsley/
  Laurence Raines*

FABRICATOR—*Pinnacle Exhibits*

FABRICATOR TEAM—*Chris Olberding*

AUDIO VISUAL—*Richenbach & Associates*

SPACE—*47,000 sq. ft.*

PHOTOGRAPHER—*Andy Caulfield, Needham Heights, MA.*

If ever an exhibit needs to "shout" to be "heard," it certainly must at the E3 show which is a "maelstrom of visual anarchy." Mauk Designs stepped into that arena with a gigantic 47,000 sq. ft. space and created this award winning design for Sony PlayStation.

To introduce the new video games to retail buyers, video game executives and video game developers, Sony PlayStation said it all with its positioning statement— "Live in your world—Play in ours." The exhibit itself, which would have 100,000 people moving about in and playing in the space, was conceived as a cityscape "in which radically different game feature areas were held together with a high tech visual glue." Elevated catwalks, 13 ft. off the ground, facilitated movement to the different areas within the mammoth space while new games were showcased on flat plasma screens on the railings along the walkways.

A pair of 15 ft. x 20 ft. LED Jumbotron monitors made up the entry portal. The main boulevard walls were made of fabric stretched over metal tube frames and the Central Crossroads Tower was composed of aluminum and frosted lexan. In the Metal Gear Solid Games feature area actual metal shipping containers were utilized— like a replay from the high tech game being replayed.

The Extreme Arena was the focal point for PlayStation's Sports Video Games. The arena, which accommodated 100 cheering fans, was constructed of thin concrete board with cast resin bolts. Expanded metal awnings and real looking arena lights added to the high-tech authenticity of the arena setting.

Another popular area was the Square Soft Theater. Seated on red metal and brocade covered opera house chairs selections from the Parasite Eve video game could be enjoyed in the opulent, baroque surround of red velvet and "dandelion" chandeliers. The exterior was made up of metal 2 in. x 4 in. studs.

27 meeting rooms were reused in other exhibits as were all of the catwalk legs and cross members. In being ecolog-ically responsible, the designer and client also reused the entire two story tech building. All the aluminum and steel was recycled and, where possible, theatrical lighting on scrim fabric was used instead of laminate or plywood walls as on the "walls" along the Main Boulevard.

SONY
PLAYSTATION

CLIENT—*Sony Computer Entertainment of America*

TRADE SHOW—*E3, 1999, Los Angeles, CA*

DESIGN—*Mauk Design , San Francisco, CA.*

DESIGN TEAM—*Mitchell Mauk/Adam Brodsley/*
Laurence Raines/James Pennington-Kent

FABRICATION—*Pinnacle Exhibits*

FABRICATION TEAM—*Chris Olberding/Rob Roth*

LIGHT—*Paul Palazzo*

AUDIO VISUAL—*Richenbach & Associates*

SPECIAL PROPS/DECORATIVES—*Dillon Works*

SPACE—*44,100 sq.ft.*

PHOTOGRAPHY—*Andy Caulfield, Needham Heights, MA*

"E3 is the loudest, cheesiest trade show on the planet. In this visual anarchy, PlayStation needed to portray their games as exciting, innovative and high quality." The challenge for Mauk Design, quoted above, was to create an entire world of PlayStation games in the midst of this chaos. They had a giant square—210 ft. x 210 ft.—to get over 100,000 persons in, around and to the games.

"The exhibit was envisioned as a cityscape in which the radically different game feature areas were held together with a high-tech visual glue." Using the city street metaphor made access into the interior easier and the elevated catwalks allowed for overhead transit to other parts of the exhibit while showcasing new games on monitors set on the railings. To bring the attendees into this "city," the designers created an eye-popping, color filled entry portal which could be seen from almost anywhere.

CATERPILLAR

CLIENT—*Caterpillar Inc.. Larry Arvin*

TRADE SHOW—*Minexpo, Las Vegas, NV*

DESIGNER—*Exhibitgroup/Giltspur, Chicago & Simantel, Exponent*

FABRICATION—*Exhibitgroup/Giltspur, Chicago*

AUDIO VISUALS—*Andy Flanagan/William Garard*

SPACE—*22500 sq.ft.*

PHOTOGRAPHY—*Jamie Padgett & Co.*

It took five days to install this monster exhibit designed by the Chicago division of Exhibitgroup/Giltspur for Caterpillar, Inc. In addition to two private, enclosed spaces and an air conditioned auditorium for feature video and live presentations, the designers included elevated walkways across the 150 ft. x 150 ft. space so that attendees could get to and from the interconnected observation platforms and the cabs of all five massive vehicles being introduced. Educational videos about mining were also shown on the raised decks.

The bright yellow vehicles dominated the floor. They were surrounded by an almost all-gray environment accented with black and an occasional shot of red. There were live demonstrations on the features and advantages of the 777 Autonomous truck which showed the truck at work at a mine site. Especially effective was the mound of "rocks" being torn up and scooped up by one Caterpillar truck while another showed the giant truck's dumpster raised up and ready to drop its contents. As a "photo op" there was a miner sculpting the Caterpillar logo out of a rock.

A 13 ft. x 8 ft. fiber-optic enhanced map graphic showed the Caterpillar dealer network as well as the company's manufacturing and distribution facilities and customer locations. In addition, adding softening elements to the rugged exhibit design were appropriate props and plantings that helped to create lifelike vignette settings for some of the vehicles. TV monitors were displayed throughout the exhibit and carried the live remote presentations as well as specially prepared videos. The designers credit the client's attention to details. They used various marketing opportunities to promote and reinforce the presence of the booth from promotional graphics and videos at the Las Vegas airport to photo key-cards at the headquarters hotel. Caterpillar also integrated dealer events at the Tucson testing grounds with the show presentations—via live remote—and they even outfitted the staff on the exhibit floor with appropriate costumes.